PHAROS AND PHARILLON

By the same Author

★

Novels

WHERE ANGELS FEAR TO TREAD
THE LONGEST JOURNEY
A ROOM WITH A VIEW
HOWARDS END
A PASSAGE TO INDIA
MAURICE

Short Stories

THE COLLECTED SHORT STORIES

Biography

GOLDWORTHY LOWES DICKINSON
THE HILL OF DEVI
MARIANNE THORNTON 1797-1887

Essays and Criticism

ASPECTS OF THE NOVEL
ABINGER HARVEST
TWO CHEERS FOR DEMOCRACY

PHAROS AND PHARILLON

E. M. FORSTER

BERKELEY: CREATIVE ARTS
1980

L. C. Catalog card number: 62-1459

ISBN 0-916870-28-6

CREATIVE ARTS BOOKS
ARE PUBLISHED BY DONALD S. ELLIS

Original copyright © 1923 and 1951 by *E. M. Forster.* Renewal copyright © 1979 by *The Provost and Scholars of King's College, Cambridge.* Creative Arts edition copyright © 1980 by Creative Arts Book Company. All rights reserved. No part of this book may be reproduced in any form without permission in writing from the publisher, except by a reviewer, who may quote brief passages in a review to be printed in a magazine or newspaper. Manufactured in the United States of America and published by
Creative Arts Book Company
833 Bancroft Way
Berkeley, California

Ἑρμῇ ψυχοπομπῷ

CONTENTS

FIVE of the following chapters are reprinted by the courtesy of *The Nation and the Athenæum*; the remainder have not been previously published in this country.

I am indebted to Mr. C. P. Cavafy for permission to publish his poems, and to Mr. George Valassopoulo for his translation of them.

—E. M. Forster

INTRODUCTION

BEFORE there was civilization in Egypt, or the delta
of the Nile had been formed, the whole country as far
south as modern Cairo lay under the sea. The shores of
this sea were a limestone desert. The coast line was
smooth usually, but at the north-west corner a remarkable spur jutted out from the main mass. It was less
than a mile wide, but thirty miles long. Its base is not
far from Bahig, Alexandria is built half-way down it,
its tip is the headland of Aboukir. On either side of it
there was once deep salt water.

Centuries passed, and the Nile, issuing out of its
crack above Cairo, kept carrying down the muds of
Upper Egypt and dropping them as soon as its current
slackened. In the north-west corner they were arrested
by this spur and began to silt up against it. It was a
shelter not only from the outer sea, but from the
prevalent wind. Alluvial land appeared; the large
shallow lake of Mariout was formed; and the current
of the Nile, unable to escape through the limestone
barrier, rounded the headland of Aboukir and entered
the outer sea by what was known in historical times as
the "Canopic" mouth.

To the north of the spur and more or less parallel to
it runs a second range of limestone. It is much shorter,
also much lower, lying mainly below the surface of the
sea in the form of reefs, but without it there would have
been no harbours (and consequently no Alexandria),
because it breaks the force of the waves. Starting at

Agame, it continues as a series of rocks across the entrance of the modern harbour. Then it re-emerges to form the promontory of Ras el Tin, disappears into a second series of rocks that close the entrance of the Eastern Harbour, and makes its final appearance as the promontory of Silsileh, after which it rejoins the big spur.

Such is the scene where the following actions and meditations take place; that limestone ridge, with alluvial country on one side of it and harbours on the other, jutting from the desert, pointing towards the Nile; a scene unique in Egypt, nor have the Alexandrians ever been truly Egyptian. Here Africans, Greeks and Jews combined to make a city; here a thousand years later the Arabs set faintly but durably the impress of the Orient; here after secular decay rose another city, still visible, where I worked or appeared to work during a recent war. Pharos, the vast and heroic lighthouse that dominated the first city—under Pharos I have grouped a few antique events; to modern events and to personal impressions I have given the name of Pharillon, the obscure successor of Pharos, which clung for a time to the low rock of Silsileh and then slid unobserved into the Mediterranean.

PHAROS

PHAROS

I

THE career of Menelaus was a series of small mishaps. It was after he had lost Helen, and indeed after he had recovered her and was returning from Troy, that a breeze arose from the north-west and obliged him to take refuge upon a desert island. It was of limestone, close to the African coast, and to the estuary though not to the exit of the Nile, and it was protected from the Mediterranean by an outer barrier of reefs. Here he remained for twenty days, in no danger, but in high discomfort, for the accommodation was insufficient for the Queen. Helen had been to Egypt ten years before, under the larger guidance of Paris, and she could not but remark that there was nothing to see upon the island and nothing to eat and that its beaches were infested with seals. Action must be taken, Menelaus decided. He sought the sky and sea, and chancing at last to apprehend an old man he addressed to him the following wingèd word:

"What island is this?"

"Pharaoh's," the old man replied.

"Pharos?"

"Yes, Pharaoh's, Prouti's,"—Prouti being another title (it occurs in the hieroglyphs) for the Egyptian king.

"Proteus?"

"Yes."

As soon as Menelaus had got everything wrong, the

wind changed and he returned to Greece with news of an
island named Pharos whose old man was called Proteus
and whose beaches were infested with nymphs. Under
such misapprehensions did it enter our geography.

Pharos was hammer-headed, and long before
Menelaus landed some unknown power—Cretan—
Atlantean—had fastened a harbour against its western
promontory. To the golden-haired king, as to us, the
works of that harbour showed only as ochreous patches
and lines beneath the dancing waves, for the island has
always been sinking, and the quays, jetties, and double
breakwater of its prehistoric port can only be touched
by the swimmer now. Already was their existence
forgotten, and it was on the other promontory—the
eastern—that the sun of history arose, never to set.
Alexander the Great came here. Philhellene, he
proposed to build a Greek city upon Pharos. But the
ridge of an island proved too narrow a site for his
ambition, and the new city was finally built upon
the opposing coast—Alexandria. Pharos, tethered to
Alexandria by a long causeway, became part of a
larger scheme and only once re-entered Alexander's
mind: he thought of it at the death of Hephæstion, as he
thought of all holy or delectable spots, and he arranged
that upon its distant shore a shrine should com-
memorate his friend, and reverberate the grief that
had convulsed Ecbatana and Babylon.

Meanwhile the Jews had been attentive. They, too,
liked delectable spots. Deeply as they were devoted to
Jehovah, they had ever felt it their duty to leave his
city when they could, and as soon as Alexandria began
to develop they descended upon her markets with

polite cries. They found so much to do that they decided against returning to Jerusalem, and met so many Greeks that they forgot how to speak Hebrew. They speculated in theology and grain, they lent money to Ptolemy the second king, and filled him (they tell us) with such enthusiasm for their religion that he commanded them to translate their Scriptures for their own benefit. He himself selected the translators, and assigned for their labours the island of Pharos because it was less noisy than the mainland. Here he shut up seventy rabbis in seventy huts, whence in an incredibly short time they emerged with seventy identical translations of the Bible. Everything corresponded. Even when they slipped they made seventy slips, and Greek literature was at last enriched by the possession of an inspired book. It was left to later generations to pry into Jehovah's scholarship and to deduce that the Septuagint translation must have extended over a long period and not have reached completion till 100 B.C. The Jews of Alexandria knew no such doubts. Every year they made holiday on Pharos in remembrance of the miracle, and built little booths along the beaches where Helen had once shuddered at the seals. The island became a second Sinai whose moderate thunders thrilled the philosophic world. A translation, even when it is the work of God, is never as intimidating as an original; and the unknown author of the "Wisdom of Solomon" shows, in his delicious but dubious numbers, how unalarming even an original could be when it was composed at Alexandria:

Let us enjoy the good things that are present, and let us speedily use the creatures like as in youth.

Let us fill ourselves with costly wine and ointments, and
let no flower of the spring pass by us.

Let us crown ourselves with rose-buds before they are
withered.

Let none of us go without his part in our voluptuousness,
let us leave tokens of our joyfulness in every place, for this is
our portion and our lot is this.

It is true that, pulling himself together, the writer
goes on to remind us that the above remarks are no
elegy on Alexander and Hephæstion, but an indictment
of the ungodly, and must be read sarcastically.

Such things they did imagine and were deceived, for their
own wickedness hath blinded them.

As for the mysteries of God they knew them not, neither
hoped they for the wages of righteousness nor discerned a
reward for blameless souls.

For God created man to be immortal, and made him to be
the image of his own eternity.

But it is too late. And all racial and religious effort
was too late. Though Pharos was not to be Greek it
was not to be Hebrew either. A more impartial power
dominated it. Five hundred feet above all shrines and
huts, Science had already raised her throne.

II

A lighthouse was a necessity. The coast of Egypt is,
in its western section, both flat and rocky, and ships
needed a landmark to show them where Alexandria lay,
and a guide through the reefs that block her harbours.
Pharos was the obvious site, because it stood in front of
the city; and on Pharos the eastern promontory, because
it commanded the more important of the two harbours—
the Royal. But it is not clear whether a divine madness

also seized the builders, whether they deliberately
winged engineering with poetry, and tried to add a
wonder to the world. At all events they succeeded, and
the arts combined with science to praise their triumph.
Just as the Parthenon had been identified with Athens,
and St. Peter's was to be identified with Rome, so,
to the imagination of contemporaries, "The Pharos"
became Alexandria and Alexandria the Pharos. Never,
in the history of architecture, has a secular building been
thus worshipped and taken on a spiritual life of its own.
It beaconed to the imagination, not only to ships, and
long after its light was extinguished memories of it
glowed in the minds of men. Perhaps it was merely very
large; reconstructions strike a chill, and the minaret, its
modern descendant, is not supremely beautiful. Something very large to which people got used—a Liberty
Statue, an Eiffel Tower? The possibility must be faced,
and is not excluded by the ecstasies of the poets.

The lighthouse was made of local limestone, of
marble, and of reddish-purple granite from Assouan. It
stood in a colonnaded court that covered most of the
promontory. There were four stories. The bottom story
was over two hundred feet high, square, pierced with
many windows. In it were the rooms (estimated at
three hundred) where the mechanics and keepers were
housed, and its mass was threaded by a spiral ascent,
probably by a double spiral. There may have been
hydraulic machinery in the central well for raising the
fuel to the top; otherwise we must imagine a procession
of donkeys who cease not night and day to circum-
ambulate the spirals with loads of wood upon their
backs. The story ended in a cornice and in statues of

Tritons: here too, in great letters of lead, was a Greek inscription mentioning the architect: "Sostratus of Cnidus, son of Dexiphanes, to the Saviour Gods: for sailors"—an inscription which, despite its simplicity, bore a double meaning. The Saviour Gods were the Dioscuri, but a courtly observer could refer them to Ptolemy Soter and his wife, whose worship their son was then promoting. For the building of the lighthouse (279 B.C.) was connected with an elaborate dynastic propaganda known as the "As-good-as-Olympic Games," and with a mammoth pageant which passed through the streets of Alexandria, regardless of imagination and expense. Nothing could be seen in the pageant, neither elephants nor camels nor dances of wild men, nor allegorical females upon a car, nor eggs that opened and disclosed the Dioscuri; and the inscription on the first story of the Pharos was a subtle echo of its appeal.

The second story was octagonal and entirely filled by the ascending spirals. The third story was circular. Then came the lantern. The lantern is a puzzle, because a bonfire and delicate scientific instruments appear to have shared its narrow area. Visitors speak, for instance, of a mysterious "mirror" up there, which was even more wonderful than the building itself. Why didn't this mirror crack, and what was it? A polished steel reflector for the fire at night or for heliography by day? Some writers describe it as made of finely wrought glass or transparent stone, and declare that when they sat under it they could see ships at sea that were invisible to the naked eye. A telescope? Is it conceivable that the Alexandrian school of mathematics and mechanics discovered the lens and that their discovery

was lost and forgotten when the Pharos fell? It is
possible: the discoveries of Aristarchus were forgotten,
and Galileo persecuted for reviving them. It is certain
that the lighthouse was equipped with every scientific
improvement known to the age, that it was the outward
expression of the studies pursued in the Museum across
the straits, and that its architect could have consulted
not only Aristarchus, but Eratosthenes, Apollonius of
Perga, and Euclid.

Standing on the lantern, at the height of five hundred
feet above the ground, a statue of Poseidon struck the
pious note, and gave a Greek air to Africa seen from
the sea. Other works of art are also reported: for
example, a statue whose finger followed the diurnal
course of the sun, a second statue who gave out with
varying and melodious voices the various hours of the
day, and a third who shouted an alarm as soon as a
hostile flotilla set sail from any foreign port. This last
must belong to an even more remarkable building, the
Pharos of legend, which we will measure in a moment.
The lighthouse was the key of the Alexandrian
defences, and Cæsar occupied it before attacking the
city. It was also the pivot of a signalling system that
stretched along the coast. Fifteen miles to the west, on a
ridge among masses of marigolds, the little watch-
tower of Abousir is still standing, and it reproduces, in
its three stories, the arrangements of Sostratus.

III

"I have taken a city," wrote the Arab conqueror of
Alexandria, "of which I can only say that it contains

4000 palaces, 4000 baths, 400 theatres, 12,000 green-
grocers, and 40,000 Jews." It contained a lighthouse,
too, for the Pharos was still perfect and functioned for a
few years more, lighting the retreating fleets of Europe
with its beams. Then a slow dissolution began, and it
shrinks, looms through the mists of legend, disappears.
The first, and the irreparable, disaster was the fall of
the lantern in the eighth century, carrying with it
scientific apparatus that could not be replaced. Annoyed
(say the Arabs) with the magic mirror that detected or
scorched their ships, the Christians made a plot, and
sent a messenger to Islam with news of a treasure in
Syria. The treasure was found, whereupon the messenger
reported something supreme—the whole wealth of
Alexander and other Pharaohs which lay in the
foundations of the lighthouse. Demolition began, and
before the Alexandrians, who knew better, could
intervene, the mirror had fallen and was smashed on
the rocks beneath. Henceforward the Pharos is only a
stump with a bonfire on the top. The Arabs made some
restorations, but they were unsubstantial additions to
the octagon, which the wind could blow away. Structural
repairs were neglected, and in the twelfth century the
second disaster occurred—the fall of the octagon
through an earthquake. The square bottom story
survived as a watch-tower. Two hundred years later it
vanished in a final earthquake, and the very island
where it had stood modified its shape and became a
peninsula, joined to the mainland by a strip of sand.

Though unable to maintain the lighthouse on earth,
the Arabs did much for it in the realms of fancy,
increasing its height to seven hundred feet, and

endowing it with various magical objects, of which the most remarkable was a glass crab. There really were crabs at Alexandria, but of copper, quite small, and standing under Cleopatra's Needle; America possesses one to-day. Oriental imagination mixed two monuments into one, and caused a Moorish army to invade the Pharos and to ride through its three hundred rooms. The entrance gate vanished, and they could not find their way out, but ever descending the spirals came at last to the glass crab, slipped through a crack in its back and were drowned. Happier, though equally obscure, was the fate of another visitor, the poet El Deraoui. Who sings:

A lofty platform guides the voyager by night, guides him with its light when the darkness of evening falls.

Thither have I borne a garment of perfect pleasure among my friends, a garment adorned with the memory of beloved companions.

On its height a dome enshadowed me, and there I saw my friends like stars.

I thought that the sea below me was a cloud, and that I had set up my tent in the midst of the heavens.

Only occasionally does the note of disillusionment and bitterness creep in. Jelaled Din ibn Mokram complains that:

The visitor to Alexandria receives nothing in the way of hospitality except some water and a description of Pompey's Pillar.

Those who make a special effort sometimes give him a little fresh air too, and tell him where the Pharos is, adding a sketch of the sea and its waves and an account of the large Greek ships.

The visitor need not aspire to receive any bread, for to an application of this type there is no reply.

As a rule, life in its shadow is an earthly ecstasy that may even touch heaven. Hark to Ibn Dukmak:

> According to the law of Moses, if a man make a pilgrimage round Alexandria in the morning, God will make for him a golden crown set with pearls, perfumed with musk and camphor and shining from the east to the west.

Nor were the Arabs content with praising the lighthouse: they even looked at it. "El Manarah", as they called it, gave the name to, and became the model for, the minaret, and one can still find minarets in Egypt that exactly reproduce the design of Sostratus—the bottom story square, second octagonal, third round.

The Fort of Kait Bey, built in the fifteenth century and itself now a ruin, stands to-day where the Pharos once stood. Its area covers part of the ancient enclosure —the rest is awash with the sea—and in its containing wall are embedded a few granite columns. Inside the area is a mosque, exactly occupying the site of the lighthouse, and built upon its foundations: here, too, are some granite blocks standing with druidical effect at the mosque's entrance. Nothing else can be attributed to the past, its stones have vanished and its spirit also. Again and again, looking at the mosque, have I tried to multiply its height by five, and thus build up its predecessor. The effort always failed: it did not seem reasonable that so large an edifice should have existed. The dominant memory in the chaos is now British, for here are some large holes, made by Admiral Seymour when he bombarded the Fort in 1882 and laid the basis of our intercourse with modern Egypt.

THE RETURN FROM SIWA

ALEXANDER THE GREAT founded Alexandria. He
came with Dinocrates, his architect, and ordered him
to build, between the sea and the lake, a magnificent
Greek town. Alexander still conceived of civilization
as an extended Greece, and of himself as a Hellene. He
had taken over Hellenism with the ardour that only a
proselyte knows. A Balkan barbarian by birth, he had
pushed himself into the enchanted but enfeebled circle
of little city states. He had flattered Athens and spared
Thebes, and preached a crusade against Persia, which
should repeat upon a vaster scale the victories of
Marathon and Salamis. He would even repeat the
Trojan war. At the Dardanelles his archæological zeal
was such that he ran naked round the tomb of Achilles.
He cut the knot of Gordius. He appeased the soul of
Priam.

Having annexed Asia Minor, Syria, Palestine, and
Egypt from the Persians, and having given his orders
to Dinocrates, he left the city he was building, and rode
with a few friends into the western desert. It was
summer. The waters of Lake Mariout, more copious
then than now, spread fertility for a space. Leaving their
zone, he struck south, over the limestone hills, and lost
sight of civilization whether of the Hellenic or non-
Hellenic type. Around him little flat pebbles shimmered
and danced in the heat, gazelles stared, and pieces of
sky slopped into the sand. Over him was the pale blue
dome of heaven, darkened, if we are to believe his

historian, by flocks of obsequious birds, who sheltered the King with their shadows and screamed when he rode the wrong way. Alexander went on till he saw below him, in the fall of the ground, the canals and hot springs and olives and palms of the Oasis of Siwa.

Sekhet-Amit the Egyptians called it, and worshipped their god Amen there, whom the Greeks call Ammon, worshipped him in the form of an emerald that lay in a sacred boat, worshipped him as a ram also. Instead of the twin mud-cities of Siwa and Aghurmi, Alexander saw pylons and colonnades, and descending into the steamy heat of the Oasis approached a lonely and mysterious shrine. For what was it mysterious? Perhaps merely for its loneliness. The distance, the solitude of the desert, touch travellers even to-day, and sharpen the imaginations of men who have crossed in armoured cars, and whom no god awaits, only a tract of green. Alexander rode, remembering how, two hundred years before him, the Persians had ridden to loot the temple, and how on them as they were eating in the desert a sandstorm had descended, burying diners and dinner in company. Herein lay the magic of Siwa. It was difficult to reach. He, being the greatest man of his epoch, had of course succeeded. He, the Philhellene, had come. His age was twenty-five. Then took place that celebrated and extraordinary episode. According to the official account the Priest came out of the temple and saluted the young tourist as Son of God. Alexander acquiesced and asked whether he would become King of this World. The reply was in the affirmative. Then his friends asked whether they should worship him. They were told that they should, and the episode closed. Some say that it is

to be explained by the Priest's bad Greek. He meant to
say Paidion ("my child") and said Paidios ("O Son of
God") instead. Others say that it never took place,
and Walter Savage Landor has imagined a conversation
in the course of which the Priest scares the King by a
snake. A scare he did get—a fright, a psychic experience,
a vision, a "turn". His development proves it. After his
return from Siwa his aspirations alter. Never again does
he regard Greece as the centre of the world.

The building of Alexandria proceeded, and copied or
magnified forms from the perishing peninsula overseas.
Dinocrates planned Greek temples and market-places,
and they were constructed not slavishly but with
intelligence, for the Greek spirit still lived. But it lived
consciously, not unconsciously as in the past. It had a
mission, and no missionary shall ever create. And
Alexander, the heroic chaos of whose heart surged with
desire for all that can and can not be, turned away from
his Hellenic town-planning and his narrow little
antiquarian crusade, and flung himself again, but in a
new spirit, against the might of Persia. He fought her
as a lover now. He wanted not to convert but to
harmonize, and conceived himself as the divine and
impartial ruler beneath whom harmony shall proceed.
That way lies madness. Persia fell. Then it was the turn
of India. Then the turn of Rome would have come and
then he could have sailed westward (such was his
expressed intention) until he had conquered the Night
and eastward until he had conquered the Day. He was
never—despite the tuition of Aristotle—a balanced
young man, and his old friends complained that in this
latter period he sometimes killed them. But to us, who

cannot have the perilous honour of his acquaintance, he grows more lovable now than before. He has caught, by the unintellectual way, a glimpse of something great, if dangerous, and that glimpse came to him first in the recesses of the Siwan Oasis. When at the age of thirty-three he died, when the expedition that he did not seek stole towards him in the summer-house at Babylon, did it seem to him as after all but the crown of his smaller quests? He had tried to lead Greece, then he had tried to lead mankind. He had succeeded in both. But was the universe also friendly, was it also in trouble, was it calling on him, on him, for his help and his love? The priest of Amen had addressed him as "Son of God". What exactly did the compliment mean? Was it explicable this side of the grave?

EPIPHANY

DURING the last years of their lives the old King and
Queen had seldom left the Palace. They sought seclusion,
though for different reasons. The King, who was gay
and shy, did not wish his pleasures to be observed. He
had gathered a suitable circle of friends round him, and
was content. There was Agathocles—who, by the way,
was Prime Minister; there was Agathoclea—who, by
the way, was the little prince's nurse; there was
Œnanthe, the mother of the two A.'s, an elderly but
accomplished woman who knew how to shampoo. And
there were one or two more, for instance the wife of a
forage contractor who would say to the King: "Here,
Daddy, drink this." The King liked young women who
called him Daddy; and he drank, and when he had drunk
enough he would get up and dance, the others danced
too, he would fall down, it was all delightful. But it was
not a delight he desired his subjects to witness.

The Queen employed herself otherwise. Shut up in
her own apartments, she meditated on the past. She
thought of all the years when she had been on trial:
the King had never cared for her, and, though negotiat-
ing for the marriage, had kept her waiting. Then came
the Battle of Rafa. The Syrians were invading Egypt,
and just as the Egyptian army was breaking she had
ridden forth among the elephants, her hair streaming,
her colour high, and had turned defeat into victory. She
became the popular heroine, and he married her. But
for nine years they had had no child. She could see no

hope anywhere. The child had come, but the situation had not changed. Months passed, and still she sat in the Palace enclosure—the Fortress inside the fortress of the Royal City—and looked from the promontory that we now call Silsileh across the harbour to Pharos, and over the unvarying expanse of the sea.

Change came at last. One night, when the King fell down, he failed to get up again. Agathoclea paid him every attention, but he passed into a stupor and died in her arms. His friends were in despair. He had been such a jolly old King. And besides, what were they to do? The Queen, on the other hand, came forward in an unexpected light. There was no occasion for anxiety, she told them. She knew what to do quite well. She was now Regent, and her first act was to dismiss the ministry. Moreover, since he was now four years old, her son no longer required a nurse. The old heroic feelings came back to her. Life seemed worth living again. She returned to her apartments full of exaltation. She entered them. As she did so, the curtains, which had been soaked with inflammable oil in her absence, burst into flame. She tried to retire. The doors had been locked behind her, and she was burnt to death.

And the life of Alexandria went on as before. Œnanthe and her progeny still drove about in the state carriages. The King and Queen still failed to appear in public, and the Palace still rose inviolate inside the walls of the Royal City. Months passed, fourteen months.

When rumours began, the A.'s neglected to act. Inertia had served them so well that they did not know how to relinquish it. But rumours continued, and after many consultations they devised a pageant that had the

feeblest effect. It was not true, they said, that the old
King and Queen had died a year ago. But it was true
that they were dead. They had died that very minute.
Alas! Woe, oh woe! Here were their urns. Their little
son was now King. Here he was. Agathocles had been
appointed Regent. Here was the will. Agathoclea—here
she was—would continue to be nurse. The people,
sceptical and sullen, watched the display, which took
place in a high gallery of the Palace, overhanging the
town. The actors made their bow, and gathering up the
exhibits retired. All went on as usual for a little longer.

It was the misgovernment of Agathocles that
brought things to a crisis: that, and the report that of
the two urns only one contained human remains: the
other, which was supposed to hold the Queen, was a
dummy. Perhaps the little boy would vanish next. They
must see him, touch him. And they stormed the Palace.
It was in vain that the Regent parleyed, threatened, or
that Agathoclea repeated that she was the royal nurse.
The soldiers joined the people, and they broke gate
after gate. At last the Regent cried, "Take him!" and,
flinging their King at them, fled. The child was already
in tears. They put him on a horse, and led it outside to
the racecourse, where were assembled more human
beings than he had ever dreamt of, who shouted
Epiphany! Epiphany! and pulled him off the horse and
made him sit on a large seat. This was the world and
he did not like it. He preferred his own little circle.
Someone cried "Shall we not punish your mother's
murderers?" He sobbed "Oh yes—oh anything," and
it was so. The Regent and his sister had hidden in the
Palace. Œnanthe had driven two miles away to the

Thesmophorion, a sanctuary near the present Nouzha Gardens. All were dragged from their retreats, tortured, and killed, the women being stripped naked first.

Such were the circumstances of the accession of Ptolemy V., surnamed Epiphanes, 204 B.C.

PHILO'S LITTLE TRIP

IT was nearly a serious tumble—more serious than he anticipated. There were six in his party, all Hebrew gentlemen of position and intelligence, such as may be seen in these days filling a first-class carriage in the Cairo express on their way up to interview the Government. In those days the Government was not at Cairo but at Rome, and the six gentlemen were on their way to interview the Emperor Caligula. Observe them in their well-appointed little yacht, slipping out of the Mohammed Ali Square, which was then under water and part of the Eastern Harbour. Their faces are pale, partly from fasting, partly from anticipation, for the passage can be rough in February. And their mission was even more poignant than cotton. It concerned their faith. Jews at Alexandria had been killed and teased, and some Gentiles had, with the connivance of the Governor, erected a bronze chariot in their principal synagogue—not even a new chariot, for the horses had no tails or feet. It was a chariot once dedicated to—O Pollution!—Cleopatra. There it stood, and the Jews did not like to throw it down. And into their smaller synagogues, smaller objects, such as portraits of the Emperor, had been thrust. It is a delicate matter to complain to an Emperor about his own portrait, but Caligula was known to be a charming and reasonable young man, and the deputation had been selected for its tact.

As they crossed the harbour, the Temple of Cæsar stood out on the right, so impressive, so brilliant, that

Philo could not repress his enthusiasm and recalled the
view in after years.

It is a piece incomparably above all others (he writes). It
stands by a most commodious harbour, wonderfully high and
large in proportion; an eminent sea mark: full of choice
paintings and statues with donatives and oblatives in
abundance; and then it is beautiful all over with gold and
silver: the model curious and regular in the disposition of
the parts, as galleries, libraries, porches, courts, halls, walks,
and consecrated groves, as glorious as expense and art could
make them, and everything in its proper place; besides that,
the hope and comfort of seafaring men, either coming in or
going out.

When would he see this temple as he came in?
Although Cleopatra had begun it for Antony, and
Augustus finished it for himself, it filled him with love,
and he turned from it with reluctance to the coast on the
left, really more important, because Jehovah had trans-
lated the entire Bible into Greek there. There stood
those seventy huts! O wonder! It was one of the
anecdotes with which he hoped to rivet the attention of
Caligula, when they arrived at Rome.

That charming and reasonable young man had lately
recovered from a severe illness, at which the whole
civilized world rejoiced, and the Eternal City was full
of embassies waiting to congratulate him. Among these,
ominously enough, was a counter-deputation from
Alexandria, strongly anti-Semite in tone. Philo watched
it narrowly. The imperial invalid did not arrive till
August, and at first things went pleasantly enough. He
caught sight of the Jews one day as he was calling on
his mother, seemed transported with delight and waved
his hand to them, also sent a message that he would

see them at once, but immediately left for Naples, and
they had to follow him thither.

It was somewhere between Naples and Baiæ that
the little trip came to its end. We cannot say where
exactly, for the reason that the Emperor received the
deputation over a considerable space of ground. He was
continually on the trot throughout the audience, and
they had to trot after him. He passed from room to
room and from villa to villa, all of which, he told them,
he had thrown open for their pleasure. They thanked
him and tried to say more. He trotted on. With him ran
the counter-deputation, and also a mob of concierges,
housekeepers, glaziers, plumbers, upholsterers and
decorators, to whom he kept flinging orders. At last
he stopped. The Jews of Alexandria approached. And
with a voice of thunder he cried: "So you are the
criminals who say I am not a God." It was shattering, it
was appalling, it was the very point they had hoped
would not be raised. For they worshipped Jehovah only.
The counter-deputation shouted with delight, and the
six Hebrew gentlemen cried in unison: "Caligula!
Caligula! do not be angry with us. We have sacrificed
for you not once but three times—first at your accession,
secondly when you were ill, thirdly when——" But
the Emperor interrupted them with merciless logic.
"Exactly. For me and not to me", and dashed off to
inspect the ladies' apartments. After him they ran,
hopeless of removing Cleopatra's chariot or of interesting him in the Septuagint. They would be lucky if they
secured their lives. He climbed up to look at a ceiling.
They climbed too. He ran along a plank; so did the
Jews. They did not speak, partly from lack of breath,

partly because they were afraid of his reply. At last,
turning in their faces, he asked: "Why don't you eat
pork?" The counter-deputation shouted again. The
Jews replied that different races ate different things,
and one of them, to carry off the situation, said
some people didn't eat lamb. "Of course they don't"
said the Emperor, "lamb is beastly." The situation
grew worse. A fit of fury had seized Caligula at the
thought of lamb and he yelled: "What are your laws? I
wish to know what your laws are!" They began to tell
him and he cried out "Shut those windows", and ran
away down a corridor. Then he turned with extraordinary gentleness and said, "I beg your pardon, what
were you saying?" They began to tell him of their laws,
and he said: "We'll have all the old pictures hung
together here I think." Stopping anew, he looked
round at his shattered train of ambassadors and artisans,
and smiling, remarked: "And these are the people who
think I am not a god. I don't blame them. I merely pity
them. They can go." Philo led his party back to
Alexandria, there to meditate on the accident that had
so spoilt their little trip: Caligula was mad.

Yet did it signify—signify in the long run? The
history of the Chosen People is full of such contre-
temps, but they survive and thrive. Six hundred years
later, when Amr took the city, he found 40,000 Jews
there. And look at them in the railway carriage now.
Their faces are anxious and eloquent of past rebuffs.
But they are travelling First.

CLEMENT OF ALEXANDRIA

WHEN the assertions that were made at one time and another in the uplands of Palestine descended from their home, and, taking the ancient caravan route, crossed the River of Egypt and approached Alexandria, they entered into a new spiritual atmosphere where they were obliged to transform themselves or to perish. The atmosphere was not hostile to the assertions, indeed it welcomed them, but it insisted that, however unphilosophic they might be, they should wear the philosophic dress, that they should take some account of the assertions that had arrived previously, should recognize the existence of libraries and museums, should approach with circumspection the souls of the rich. Under these conditions they might remain. And exactly the same thing happened on two distinct occasions. We are here concerned with the second of the occasions, but it is convenient to glance at the first; it was soon after Alexandria had been founded, and Jews were flocking to her markets. An unexpected problem confronted them. Jehovah had said "I Am that I Am," and so long as they remained in Palestine this seemed enough. But now they had to face disquieting comments, such as "This statement predicates existence merely" or "This statement, while professing merely to predicate existence, assumes the attribute of speech," and they grew aware of the inaccessibility and illogicality of their national God. The result was a series of attempts on their part to explain and recommend Jehovah to the

Greeks—culminating in the great system of Philo, who, by the doctrine of the Mediating Logos, ensured that the deity should be at the same time accessible and inaccessible: "The Logos," he writes, "dwells on the margin between the Created and the Increate, and delights to serve them both." And there, for a little, the matter rested.

But in Philo's own lifetime a second assertion had been made among the Judæan hills. We do not know its original form—too many minds have worked over it since—but we know that it was unphilosophic and antisocial. For it was addressed to the uneducated and it promised them a kingdom. Following the usual route, it reached Alexandria, where the same fate overtook it: it had to face comments, and in so doing was transformed. It too evolved a system which, though not logical, paid the lip service to logic that a great city demands, and interspersed bridges of argument among the flights of faith. All Greek thinkers, except Socrates, had done the same, so that, on its intellectual side, the new religion did not break with the past; it consisted of an assertion in a philosophic dress, and Clement of Alexandria, its first theologian, used methods that were familiar to Philo two hundred years before. Not only did he bring allegory to bear upon the more intractable passages of Scripture, but he adapted the Philonian Logos and identified it with the Founder of the new religion. "In the beginning was the Word and the Word was with God." Philo might have written this. St. John had added to it two statements distinctly Christian, namely, "The Word was God" and "The Word was made flesh." And now Clement, taking over the completed conception, raised upon it a storied fabric such as the Alexandrians loved, and ensured that the deity should be at the same time accessible and inaccessible, merciful and just, human and divine. The fabric would have bewildered the fishermen of Galilee, and it had in it a flaw which became evident in the fourth century and produced the Arian schism. But it impressed the passing age; Clement, working in and through Alexandria, did more than even St. Paul to recommend Christianity to the Gentiles.

He was probably born in Greece about 150 A.D. and initiated into Mysteries there. Then he was converted and became head of the theological college in Alexandria, where he remained until his exile in 202. But little is known of his life and nothing of his character, though one may assume it was conciliatory: Christianity was not yet official, and thus in no position to fulminate. Of his treatises the "Exhortation to the Greeks" acknow-ledges several merits in pagan thought, while "The Rich Man's Salvation" handles with delicacy a problem on which business men are naturally sensitive, and arrives at the comforting conclusion that Christ did not mean what He said. One recognizes the wary resident. And when he attacks Paganism he seldom denounces: he mocks, knowing this to be the better way. For the age is literal. It had lost resilience and spring, and if one pointed out to it that Zeus had behaved absurdly in Homer, it could summon no rush of instinct or of poetry with which to defend his worship. Demeter too! And shrines to the sneezing Apollo and to the gouty and to the coughing Artemis! Ha! Ha! Fancy believing in a goddess with the gout. Clement makes great play with such nonsense. For a new religion has, as far as persiflage

is concerned, an advantage over an old one: it has not
had time itself to evolve a mythology, and his adversaries
could not retort with references to St. Simeon Stylites,
or to the plague spot of St. Roch, or to St. Fina who
allowed a devil to throw her mother down the stairs.
They could only hang their heads and assent, and when
Clement derided the priests in the idol-temples for their
dirt, they could not foresee that in the following century
dirt would be recommended as holy by the Church.
They were caught by his genial air and by his "logic";
there is nothing morose about the treatises, and even
to-day they are readable, though not quite in the way
that the author intended.

A solemn assembly of Greeks, held in honour of a dead
serpent, was gathering at Pytho, and Eunomus sang a
funeral ode for the reptile. Whether his song was a hymn in
praise of the snake or a lamentation over it, I cannot say;
but there was a competition and Eunomus was playing the
lyre in the heat of the day, at the time when the grasshoppers,
warmed by the sun, were singing under the leaves along the
hills. They were singing, you see, not to the dead serpent of
Pytho, but to the all-wise God, a spontaneous song, better
than the measured strains of Eunomus. A string breaks in
the Locrian's hands; the grasshopper settles upon the neck of
the lyre and begins to twitter there as if upon a branch: whereupon the minstrel, by adapting his music to the grasshopper's
lay, supplied the place of the missing string. So it was not
Eunomus that drew the grasshopper by his song, as the legend
would have it, when it set up the bronze figure at Pytho,
showing Eunomus with his lyre and his ally in the contest.
No, the grasshopper flew of its own accord, and sang of its
own accord, although the Greeks thought it to have been
responsive to music.

How in the world is it that you have given credence to
worthless legends, imagining . . .

and blasts of theology ensue. But how grateful one is to
Clement for mentioning the grasshopper, and how
probable it seems, from the way he tells the story, that
he had a faint consciousness of its beauty—just as his
risqué passages emanate a furtive consciousness of their
riskiness. His learning is immense: he is said to allude
to three hundred Greek writers of whom we should not
otherwise have heard, and one gladly follows him
through the back-yards of the Classical world. The
results of his ramble are most fully stated in two other
of his treatises, the "Rug roll" and the "Tutor". His
verdict is that, though the poetry of Hellas is false and
its cults absurd or vile, yet its philosophers and grasshoppers possessed a certain measure of divine truth;
some of the speculations of Plato, for instance, had been
inspired by the Psalms. It is not much of a verdict in the
light of modern research; but it is a moderate verdict
for a Father; he spares his thunders, he does not exalt
asceticism, he is never anti-social.

Till the ground if you are a husbandman; but recognize
God in your husbandry. Sail the sea, you who love sea-faring;
but ever call upon the heavenly pilot. Were you a soldier on
campaign when the knowledge of God laid hold of you? Then
listen to the commander who signals righteousness.

Here he shows his respect for the existing fabric and
his hope that it may pass without catastrophe from
Pagan to Christian, a hope that could have found
expression only at Alexandria, where contending
assertions have so often been harmonized, and whose
own god, Serapis, had expressed the union of Egypt and
Greece.

Looking back—it is so easy now to look back!—one

can see that the hope was vain. Christianity, though she
contained little that was fresh doctrinally, yet descended
with a double-edged sword that hacked the ancient
world to pieces. For she had declared war against two
great forces—Sex and the State—and during her
complicated contest with them the old order was bound
to disappear. The contest had not really begun in
Clement's day. Sex disquieted him, but he did not revolt
against it like his successor Origen. The State exiled
him, but it had not yet put forth, as it did under
Diocletian, its full claims to divinity. He lived in a
period of transition, and in Alexandria. And in that
curious city, which had never been young and hoped
never to grow old, conciliation must have seemed more
possible than elsewhere, and the graciousness of Greece
not quite incompatible with the Grace of God.

ST. ATHANASIUS

I

THAT afternoon was one of comparative calm for the infant Church. She was three hundred and ten years old. The pagan persecutions had ceased, and disputes about the Nature of Christ, over which blood was more freely to flow, had not yet matured. It still seemed that under her inspired guidance the old world would pass without disaster into the new. What lovely weather! The month was June, and the beacon of smoke that rose from the summit of the Pharos was inclined over Alexandria by a northerly wind. Both harbours were filled with ships; the Eastern Harbour was lined with palaces. The Western Harbour—and to it we must turn—was indeed less splendid. Then, as now, it washed the business quarter, the warehouses, the slums where the dock hands lived. Hardness and poverty edged it as they do to-day, and Christianity had settled here early, as she settled on all spots where the antique civilization had failed to make men dignified. Issuing out of the Gate of the Moon, the great Canopic Way here lost its straightness and split into ignoble lanes. There was only one redeeming feature—a house in which a real bishop was sitting. His name was Alexander. He has invited some clergymen to lunch, and they are late.

Bishops existed then in a profusion we can scarcely conceive. Every large village produced one, and they even went so far as to disorganize the postal service by galloping about in troops upon the government horses.

But he of Alexandria was a bishop of no ordinary brand. He bore the title of "Patriarch of all the Preaching of St. Mark," and a prestige that only Rome challenged. If he lived in these slums, it was because historical associations detained him. The sainted shoemaker Annianus had plied his trade hard by. A church to the right—St. Theonas'—had been built by another local saint. Here were the origins of his power, but its field lay elsewhere—eastward among the splendours of the town; southward, hundreds of miles southward, up the valley of the Nile. The whole of Egypt was ripe for Christianity. A magnificent prize!

The waters of the harbour, placid and slightly stale, came almost up to his house. He gazed at them, and at the grubby beach where some little boys were playing. They were playing at going to church. They were poor, they had no toys, and, since railway trains did not exist, going to church was the only game they could command. Indeed, it is a fascinating game. Even Anglican nurseries have succumbed to it. Scantily robed, they processed and inclined, and the Bishop being not Anglican, but, African, only smiled. Boys will be boys! He was specially diverted by their leader, a skinny but sportive youth, who would take his flock for a swim and, diving, reappear when and where they least expected. Then more solemn thoughts returned.

The whole of Egypt was ripe for Christianity. Ah, but for what kind of Christianity? That was the trouble. Fancy if, with Arius, it adopted the heresy of "Time was when He was not." Fancy if it paltered with Gnosticism, and believed that creation, with its palaces and slums, is the result of a muddle! Fancy if it

Judaized with Meletius, the disobedient Bishop of
Assiout! Alexander had written to Meletius, asking
him to Judaize less, but had had no reply. That was the
disadvantage of a copious episcopy. You could never
be sure that all the bishops would do the same thing.
And there were dreadful examples in which flighty lay-
men had lost their heads, and, exclaiming, "Me be
bishop too!" had run away into the desert before any
one could stop them. The Emperor Constantine (that
lion-hearted warrior!) was a further anxiety. Constantine so easily got mixed. Immersed in his town-
planning, he might stamp some heresy as official and
then the provinces would take it up. How difficult everything was! What was to be done? Perhaps the clergymen, when they arrived for lunch, would know. There
used to be too little Christianity. Now there almost
seemed too much. Alexander sighed, and looked over
the harbour to the Temple of Neptune that stood on the
promontory. He was growing old. Where was his
successor?—someone who . . . not exactly saintliness
and scholarship, but someone who would codify, would
define?

Stop! stop! Boys will be boys, but there are limits.
They were playing at Baptism now, and the sportive
youth was in the act of pouring some of the harbour
water over two other Gippoes. To enter into the
Bishop's alarm we must remember the difference
between Northern and Southern conceptions of impiety.
To the Northerner impiety is bad taste. To the
Southerner it is magic—the illicit and accurate perform-
ance of certain acts, and especially of sacramental acts.
If the youth had made any mistake in his baptismal

ritual it would not have mattered, it would have
remained play. But he was performing accurately what
he had no right to perform; he was saying, "Me be
bishop too," and Heaven alone knew the theological
consequences. "Stop! stop!" the genuine article cried.
It was too late. The water fell, the trick was done . . .
and at the same moment the clergymen arrived, offering
such apologies for their unpunctuality as are usual
among Egyptians.

It was long before lunch was served. The culprits
were summoned, and in terrific conclave their conduct
was discussed. There was some hope that the two
converts were Christians already, in which case nothing
would have been affected. But no. They had bowed the
knee to Neptune hitherto. Then were they Christians
now? Or were they horrid little demons who, outside
or inside the Church, would harm her equally? The
sportive youth prevailed. He won over the Bishop, and
calmed the clergymen's fears, and before evening fell
and the smoke on the Pharos turned to a column of fire,
it was settled that he had by his play rendered two souls
eligible for immortal bliss. And his action had a more
immediate consequence: he never washed again. Taken
into the Bishop's house, he became his pupil, his deacon,
his coadjutor, his successor in the see, and finally a saint
and a doctor of the Church: he is St. Athanasius.

II

At the other end of the city there lived another clergy-
man. His name was Arius, and it was a very long time
indeed since the Bishop had asked him to lunch. He took

duty at St. Mark's, a small church that stood on the
brink of the Mediterranean. The neighbourhood was of
the best—palaces, zoological gardens, lecture-rooms,
etc.—and over some trees rose the long back of the
temple that Cleopatra had built to Antony. That temple
would make a seemly cathedral, Arius often thought,
and the obelisks in its forecourt—Cleopatra's Needles—
would be improved if they supported statues of God the
Father. The whole of Egypt was ripe for Christianity—
for the right kind of Christianity, that is to say: not for
the kind that was preached at the western end of the town.

Arius was elderly by now. Learned and sincere, tall,
simple in his dress, persuasive in his manner, he was
accused by his enemies of looking like a snake and
of seducing, in the theological sense, seven hundred
virgins. The accusation amazed him. He had only
preached what is obviously true. Since Christ is the Son
of God, it follows that Christ is younger than God, and
that there must have been a condition—no doubt before
time began—when the First Person of the Trinity
existed, and the Second did not. This has only to be
stated to be believed, and only those who were entirely
possessed by the devil, like doddering Alexander and
slippery Athanasius, would state the contrary. The
Emperor Constantine (that lion-hearted warrior!)
would certainly see the point, provided it was explained
to him. But Constantine so easily got mixed, and there
was indeed a danger that he would stamp the wrong
type of Christianity as official, and plunge the world into
heresy for thousands of years. How difficult everything
was! One's immediate duty was to testify, so day after
day Arius preached Arianism to the seven hundred

virgins, to the corpse of the Evangelist St. Mark who lay buried beneath the church, and to the bright blue waves of the sea that in their ceaseless advance have now covered the whole scene.

The quarrel between him and his bishop grew so fierce and spread so far that Constantine was obliged to intervene and to beg his fellow-Christians to imitate the Greek philosophers, who could differ without shedding one another's blood. It was just the sort of appeal that everyone had been fearing that the Emperor would make. He was insufficiently alive to eternal truth. No one obeyed, and in desperation he summoned them to meet him at Nicæa on the Black Sea, and spent the interval in trying to find out what their quarrel turned on. Two hundred and fifty bishops attended, many priests, deacons innumerable. Among the last named was Athanasius, who, thundering against Arius in full conclave, procured his overthrow. Amid scenes of incredible violence the Nicene Creed was passed, containing clauses (since omitted) in which Arianism was anathematized. Arius was banished. Athanasius led his tottering but triumphant bishop back to Alexandria, and the Emperor returned to the town-planning and to the wardrobes of wigs and false hair that sometimes solace the maturity of a military man.

The powers of Athanasius were remarkable. Like Arius, he knew what truth is, but, being a politician, he knew how truth can best be enforced; his career blends subtlety with vigour, self-abnegation with craft. Physically he was blackish, but active and strong. One recognizes a modern street type. Not one single generous action by him is recorded, but he knew how to inspire enthusiasm, and before he died had become a popular hero and set the pace to his century. Soon after his return from Nicæa he was made Patriarch of Alexandria, but he had scarcely sat down before Arius was back there too. The Emperor wished it. Could not Christians imitate, etc. . . . ? No; Christians could not and would not; and Athanasius testified with such vigour that he was banished in his turn, and his dusty theological Odyssey begins. He was banished in all five times. Sometimes he hid in a cistern, or in pious ladies' houses, or in the recesses of the Libyan desert; at other times, going farther afield, he popped up in Palestine or France. Roused by his passage from older visions, the soul of the world began to stir, and to what activity! Heavy Romans, dreamy Orientals and quick Greeks all turned to theology, and scrambled for the machinery of the Pagan State, wrenching this way and that until their common heritage was smashed. Cleopatra's temple to Antony first felt the killing glare of truth. Arians and Orthodox competed for its consecration, and in the space of six years its back was broken and its ribs cracked by fire. St. Theonas'—the episcopal church —was gutted, and Athanasius nearly killed by some soldiers on its altar. And all the time everyone was writing—encyclicals as to the date of Easter, animadversions against washing, accusations of sorcery, complaints that Athanasius had broken a chalice in a church in a village near Lake Mariout, replies that there was no chalice to break, because there was no church, because there was no village—reams and reams of paper on this subject travelling over the empire for years, and being perused by bishops in Mesopotamia and Spain. Constantine died; but his successors, whatever their faith, were drawn into the dance of theology, none more so than Julian, who dreamed of Olympus. Arius died, falling down in the streets of Alexandria one evening while he was talking to a friend; but Arianism survived. Athanasius died too; but not before he had weaned the Church from her traditions of scholarship and tolerance, the tradition of Clement and Origen. Few divines have done more for her, and her gratitude has been both profound and characteristic; she has coupled his name to a Creed with which he had nothing to do—the Athanasian.

Were his activities all about nothing? No! The Arian controversy enshrined a real emotion. By declaring that Christ was younger than God Arius tended to make him lower than God, and consequently to bring him nearer to man—indeed, to level him into a mere good man and to forestall Unitarianism. This appealed to the untheologically-minded—to Emperors, and particularly to Empresses. It made them feel less lonely. But Athanasius, who viewed the innovation with an expert eye, saw that while it popularized Christ it isolated God, and raised man no nearer to heaven in the long run. Therefore he fought it. Of the theatre of this ancient strife no trace remains in Alexandria. Not even Cleopatra's Needle stands there now. But the strife still continues in the heart of men, ever prone to substitute the human for the divine, and it is probable that many an individual Christian to-day is an Arian without knowing it.

TIMOTHY THE CAT
AND TIMOTHY WHITEBONNET

"Miaou!"

Such was the terrible sound which, half way through the fifth century, disturbed the slumbers of certain Monophysite monks. Their flesh crept. Moved by a common impulse, each stole from his cell, and saw, in the dimly lighted corridor, a figure even more mysterious than pussy's—something that gibbered and bowed and said, in hollow and sepulchral tones, "Consecrate Timothy." They stood motionless until the figure disappeared, then ran this way and that in search of it. There was nothing to be seen. They opened the convent doors. Nothing to be seen except Alexandria glimmering, still entirely marble; nothing except the Pharos, still working and sending out from the height of five hundred feet a beam visible over a radius of seventy miles. The streets were quiet, owing to the absence of the Greek garrison in Upper Egypt. Having looked at the tedious prospect, the monks withdrew, for much had to be done before morning: they had to decide whether it was an angel or a devil who had said "Miaou." If the former, they must do penance for their lack of faith; if the latter, they were in danger of hell-fire. While they argued over a point that has puzzled the sharpest of saints, the attention of some of them began to wander, and to dwell on one who was beyond doubt a devil—Proterius, whom the Emperor had imposed on them as their Patriarch, and who slept in a convent hard

by. They cursed Proterius. They reflected too that in
the absence of the garrison he no longer slept safely,
that they were Egyptians and numerous, he a Greek
and alone. They cursed him again, and the apparition
reappeared repeating, "Consecrate Timothy." Timothy
was one of their own number and the holiest of men.
When, after an interval, they ran to his cell, they found
him upon his knees in prayer. They told him of the
ghostly message, and he seemed dazed, but on collecting
himself implored that it might never be mentioned again.
Asked whether it was infernal, he refused to reply.
Asked whether it was supernal, he replied, "You, not I,
have said so." All doubts disappeared, and away they
ran to find some bishops. Melchite or Arian or Sabæan
or Nestorian or Donatist or Manichæan bishops would
not do: they must be Monophysite. Fortunately two
had occurred, and on the following day Timothy,
struggling piously, was carried between Cleopatra's
Needles into the cathedral and consecrated Patriarch of
Alexandria and of all the Preaching of St. Mark. For he
held the correct opinion as to the Nature of Christ—the
only possible opinion: Christ has a single Nature, divine,
which has absorbed the human: how could it be otherwise? The leading residential officials, the municipal
authorities, and the business community thought the
same; so, attacking Proterius, who thought the contrary, they murdered him in the Baptistery, and hanged
him over the city wall. The Greek garrison hurried
back, but it was too late. Proterius had gone, nor did the
soldiers regret him, for he had made more work than
most bishops, having passed the seven years of his
episcopate in a constant state of siege. Timothy, for

whom no guards need be set, was a great improvement. Diffident and colloquial, he won everyone's heart, and obtained, for some reason or other, the surname of the Cat.

Thus the *coup d'église* had succeeded for the moment. But it had to reckon with another monk, a second Timothy, of whom, as events proved, the angel had really been thinking. He was Timothy Whitebonnet, so called from his headgear, and his life was more notable than the Cat's, for he lived at Canopus, where the air is so thick with demons that only the most robust of Christians can breathe. Canopus stood on a promontory ten miles east of Alexandria, overlooking the exit of the Nile. Foul influences had haunted it from the first. Helen, a thousand years ago, had come here with Paris on their flight towards Troy, and though the local authorities had expelled her for vagabondage, the ship that carried her might still be seen, upon summer nights, ploughing the waves into fire. In her train had followed Herodotus, asking idle questions of idle men; Alexander, called the Great from his enormous horns; and Serapis, a devil worse than any, who, liking the situation, had summoned his wife and child and established them on a cliff to the north, within sound of the sea. The child never spoke. The wife wore the moon. In their honour the Alexandrians used to come out along the canal in barges and punts, crowned with flowers, robed in gold, and singing spells of such potency that the words remained, though the singers were dead, and would slide into Timothy White-bonnet's ear, when the air seemed stillest, and pretend to him that they came from God. Often, just as a sentence was completed, he would realize its origin, and have to expectorate it in the form of a toad—a dangerous exercise, but it taught him discernment, and fitted him to play his part in the world. He learned with horror of the riots in the metropolis, and of the elevation of the heretical Cat. For he knew that Christ has two Natures, one human, the other divine: how can it be otherwise?

At Constantinople there seems to have been a little doubt. Leo, the reigning emperor, was anxious not to drive Egypt into revolt, and disposed to let Alexandria follow the faith she preferred. But his theologians took a higher line, and insisted on his sending a new garrison. This was done, the Cat was captured, and Whitebonnet dragged from Canopus and consecrated in his place. There matters rested until the accession of Basiliscus, who sent a new garrison to expel Whitebonnet. Once more the Cat ruled bloodily until the Emperor Zeno took the other view, and sending a——

However, the curtain may drop now. The controversy blazed for two hundred years, and is smouldering yet. The Copts still believe, with Timothy the Cat, in the single Nature of Christ; the double Nature, upheld by Timothy Whitebonnet, is still maintained by the rest of Christendom and by the reader. The Pharos, the Temple of Serapis—these have perished, being only stones, and sharing the impermanence of material things. It is ideas that live.

THE GOD ABANDONS ANTONY

When at the hour of midnight
an invisible choir is suddenly heard passing
with exquisite music, with voices—
Do not lament your fortune that at last subsides,
your life's work that has failed, your schemes that have
proved illusions.
But like a man prepared, like a brave man,
bid farewell to her, to Alexandria who is departing.
Above all, do not delude yourself, do not say that it is a
dream,
that your ear was mistaken.
Do not condescend to such empty hopes.
Like a man for long prepared, like a brave man,
like the man who was worthy of such a city,
go to the window firmly,
and listen with emotion
but not with the prayers and complaints of the coward
(Ah! supreme rapture!)
listen to the notes, to the exquisite instruments of the
mystic choir,
and bid farewell to her, to Alexandria whom you are
losing.

C. P. Cavafy.*

* For a study of Cavafy's work see p. 91.

PHARILLON

ELIZA IN EGYPT

W H E N the lively and somewhat spiteful Mrs. Eliza Fay
landed at Alexandria in the summer of 1779 that city
was at her lowest ebb. The glories of the antique had
gone, the comforts of the modern had not arrived. Gone
were the temples and statues, gone the palace of
Cleopatra and the library of Callimachus, the Pharos
had fallen and been succeeded by the feeble Pharillon,
the Heptastadion had silted up; while the successors to
these—the hotels, the clubs, the drainage system, the
exquisite Municipal buildings—still slept in the un-
astonished womb of time.

Attached to Mrs. Fay was her husband, an in-
competent advocate, who was to make their fortunes in
the East. Since the boat that had brought them was
owned by a Christian, they were forbidden to enter the
Western Harbour, and had to disembark not far from
the place where, in more enlightened days, the Ramleh
Tramway was to terminate. All was barbarism then,
save for two great obelisks, one prone, one erect—
"Cleopatra's Needles", not yet transferred to New York
and London respectively. They were met in this lonely
spot by the Prussian Consul, a certain Mr. Brandy, who
found them rooms, but had bad news for them; "a
melancholy story" as Mrs. Fay calls it when writing
to her sister. Between Cairo and Suez, on the very route
they proposed to take, a caravan had been held up and
some of its passengers murdered. She was pitiably

agitated. But she did not give up her sight-seeing; she had got to Alexandria and meant to enjoy it. Cleopatra's Needles in the first place. What did the hieroglyphics on them signify? She applied to Mr. Brandy; but the Consul, following the best traditions of the residential Levant, "seemed to know no more than ourselves." His kindness was unfailing. Next day he produced donkeys—being Christians they were not allowed to ride horses—and the party trotted over three miles of desert to Pompey's Pillar, preceded by a janissary with a drawn sword. Pompey's Pillar arouses few emotions in the modern breast. The environs are squalid, the turnstile depressing, and one knows that it dates not from Pompey but from Diocletian. Mrs. Fay approached it in a nobler mood.

Although quite unadorned, the proportions are so exquisite that it must strike every beholder with a kind of awe, which softens into melancholy when one reflects that the renowned hero, whose name it bears, was treacherously murdered on this very coast by the boatmen who were conveying him to Alexandria. His wretched wife stood on the vessel he had just left, watching his departure, as we may very naturally suppose, with inexpressible anxiety. What must have been her agonies at the dreadful event!

The time was to come when Mrs. Fay herself would have watched with very little anxiety the murder of Mr. Fay. Her Anthony—for such was his name—led her from mess to mess, and in the end she had to divorce him. Let us turn from these serious themes to a "ludicrous accident" that befell Mr. Brandy on the way to "Cleopatra's Palace". He was very large and stout, and his donkey, seizing its opportunity, stole away from under the consular seat and left him astride on the sand!

As for "Cleopatra's Palace", it was not the genuine palace, but it was as genuine as the emotion it inspired.

Never do I remember being so affected by a like object. I stood in the midst of the ruins, meditating on the awful scene, till I could have almost fancied I beheld its former mistress, revelling in luxury with her infatuated lover, Mark Anthony, who for her sake lost all.

An account of a party at the Brandies' concludes the letter—a clear-cut malicious account. Eliza is the child of her century, which affected lofty emotions but whose real interest lay in little things, and in satire.

We were most graciously received by Mrs. Brandy, who is a native of this place; but as she could speak a little Italian we managed to carry on something like a conversation. She was most curiously bedizened on the occasion, and being short, dark-complexioned, and of a complete dumpling shape, appeared altogether the strangest lump of finery I ever beheld. She had a handkerchief bound round her head, covered with strings composed of spangles, but very large, intermixed with pearls and emeralds; her neck and bosom were ornamented in the same way. Add to all this an embroidered girdle with a pair of gold clasps, I think very nearly four inches square, enormous ear-rings, and a large diamond sprig at the top of her forehead, and you must allow that she was a most brilliant figure. They have a sweet little girl about seven years of age, who was decked out in much the same style; but she really looked pretty in spite of her incongruous finery. On the whole, though, I was pleased with both mother and child; their looks and behaviour were kind, and to a stranger in a strange land (and this is literally so to us) a little attention is soothing and consolatory; especially when one feels surrounded by hostilities, which every European must do here. Compared with the uncouth beings who govern this country, I felt at home among the natives of France, and I will even say of Italy.

On taking leave, our host presented a book containing certificates of his great politeness and attentions towards travellers, which were signed by many persons of consideration, and at the same time requesting that Mr. Fay and myself would add our names to the list. We complied, though not without surprise that a gentleman in his situation should have recourse to such an expedient, which cannot but degrade him in the eyes of his guests.

Rather cattish, that last remark, considering how much the Consul had done for her. But a cat she is—spirited and observant, but a cat.

II

Heedless of the weather, heedless of the rumour of plundered caravans, Eliza removed her husband as soon as possible for the interior, and some account must now be given of their adventures. Her pen is our guide. Through flood and blood it keeps its way, curbed only by her fear of the Turkish Censor, and by her desire to conceal her forebodings from friends at home. As soon as misfortunes have occurred she will describe them. But about the future she is always confident and bright, and this gallant determination to make the best of trouble gives charm to a character that is otherwise unsympathetic.

The Fays selected the river route. Since the Mahmoudieh Canal had not been cut, they had to reach the Rosetta mouth of the Nile by sea. They were nearly drowned crossing its bar, and scarcely were they through when a boat of thieves shot out from the bank and caused Mr. Fay to fire off two pistols at once. They outsailed their pursuers, and sped up the lower reach to

Rosetta, then a more important place than Alexandria and apparently a tidier place. Eliza was delighted. Thoughts of England and of the English Bible at once welled up in her mind.

There is an appearance of cleanliness in Rosetta, the more gratifying because seldom met with in any degree so as to remind us of what we are accustomed to at home. The landscape around was interesting from its novelty, and became peculiarly so on considering it as the country where the children of Israel sojourned. The beautiful, I may say the unparalleled story of Joseph and his brethren rose to my mind as I surveyed these banks on which the Patriarch sought shelter for his old age, where his self-convicted sons bowed down before their younger brother, and I almost felt as if in a dream, so wonderful appeared the circumstance of my being here.

It is news that Jacob ever resided in the province of Behera. Passing by this, and by the Pyramids which they only saw from a distance, we accompany the Fays to Boulac, "the port of Grand Cairo", where their troubles increased. Restrictions against Christians being even severer here than at Alexandria, Mrs. Fay had to dress as a native before she might enter the city. "I had in the first place a pair of trousers with yellow leather half-boots and slippers over them"; then a long satin gown, another gown with short sleeves, a robe of silk like a surplice, muslin from her forehead to her feet, and over everything a piece of black silk. "Thus equipped, stumbling at every step, I sallied forth, and with great difficulty got across my noble beast; but as the veil prevented me breathing freely I must have died by the way." She rode into the European enclave where terror and confusion greeted her. The rumour about

the caravan proved only too true. Complete details had
just arrived. It had been plundered between Cairo and
Suez, its passengers had been killed or left to die in the
sun, and, worse still, the Turkish authorities were so
upset by the scandal that they proposed murdering the
whole of the European community in case the news
leaked out. It was thought that Mrs. Fay might be safe
with an Italian doctor. As she waddled across to his
house her veil slipped down so that a passer reprimanded
her severely for indecency. Also she fell ill.

There broke out a severe epidemical disease with violent
symptoms. People are attacked at a moment's warning with
dreadful pains in stiff limbs, a burning fever with delirium
and a total stoppage of perspiration. During two days it
increases, on the third there comes on uniformly a profuse
sweat (pardon the expression) with vomiting which carries
all off.

But as soon as her disease culminated, out she sallied
to see the ceremonies connected with the rise of the
Nile. They disappointed and disgusted her.

Not a decent person could I distinguish among the whole
group. So much for this grand exhibition, which we have
abundant cause to wish had not taken place, for the vapours
arising from such a mass of impurity have rendered the heat
more intolerable than ever. My bedchamber overlooks the
canal, so that I enjoy the full benefit to be derived from its
proximity.

Events by now were taking a calmer turn. Mr. Fay,
who had also had the epidemic, was restored to such
vitality as he possessed, and the Turkish authorities
had been persuaded by a bribe of £3000 to overcome
their sensitiveness and to leave the European colony

alive. The terrible journey remained, but beyond it lay
India and perhaps a fortune.

III

The Suez caravan—an immense affair—was formed
up in the outskirts of Cairo. In view of the recent
murders it included a large guard, and the journey,
which took three days, passed off without disaster. Mr.
Fay had a horse; Eliza, still panting in her Oriental
robes, travelled in a litter insecurely hung between two
restive camels. Peeping out through its blinds she could
see the sun and the rocks by day, and the stars by night.
She notes their beauty, her senses seem sharpened by
danger, and she was to look back on the desert with a
hint of romance. Above her head, attached to the roof
of the litter, were water-bottles, melons, and hard-
boiled eggs, her provision for the road, rumbling and
crashing together to the grave disturbance of her sleep.
"Once I was saluted by a parcel of hard eggs breaking
loose from their net and pelting me completely. It was
fortunate that they were boiled, or I should have been in
a pretty trim." By her side rode her husband, and near
him was a melancholy figure, followed by a sick greyhound, young Mr. Taylor, who became so depressed by
the heat that he slid off his horse and asked to be allowed
to die. His request was refused, as was his request that
she should receive the greyhound into her litter. Eliza
was ever sensible. She was not going to be immured
with a boiling hot dog which might bite her. "I hope no
person will accuse me of inhumanity for refusing to
receive an animal in that condition: self-preservation

forbade my compliance; I felt that it would be weakness instead of compassion to subject myself to such a risk." Consequently the greyhound died. An Arab despatched him with his scimitar, Mr. Taylor protested, the Arab ran at Mr. Taylor. "You may judge from this incident what wretches we were cast among."

They found a boat at Suez and went on board at once. Mr. Fay writes a line to his father-in-law to tell him that they are safe thus far: a grandiose little line:

Some are now very ill, but I stood it as well as any Arabian in the caravan, which consisted of at least five thousand people. My wife insists on taking the pen out of my hands.

She takes it, to the following effect:

My dear Friends—I have not a moment's time, for the boat is waiting, therefore can only beg that you will unite with me in praising our Heavenly Protector for our escape from the various dangers of our journey. I never could have thought my constitution was so strong. I bore the fatigues of the desert like a lion. We have been pillaged of almost everything by the Arabs. This is the Paradise of thieves, I think the whole population may be divided into two classes of them: those who adopt force and those who effect their purpose by fraud. . . . I have not another moment. God bless you! Pray for me, my beloved friends.

It is not clear when the Fays had been pillaged, or of what; perhaps they had merely suffered the losses incidental to an Oriental embarkation. The ship herself had been pillaged, and badly. She had been connected with the earlier caravan—the ill-fated one—and the Government had gutted her in its vague embarrassment. Not a chair, not a table was left. Still they were thankful to be on board. Their cabin was good, the captain appeared good-natured and polite, and their fellow-

passengers, a Mr. and Mrs. Tulloch, a Mr. Hare, a
Mr. Fuller, and a Mr. Manesty, seemed, together with
poor Mr. Taylor from the caravan, to promise in-
offensive companionship down the Red Sea. Calm was
the prospect. But Eliza is Eliza. And we have not yet
seen Eliza in close contact with another lady. Nor have
we yet seen Mrs. Tulloch.

IV

The beauty of the Gulf of Suez—and surely it is most
beautiful—has never received full appreciation from the
traveller. He is in too much of a hurry to arrive or to
depart, his eyes are too ardently bent on England or on
India for him to enjoy that exquisite corridor of tinted
mountains and radiant water. He is too much occupied
with his own thoughts to realize that here, here and
nowhere else, is the vestibule between the Levant and
the Tropics. Nor was it otherwise in the case of Mrs.
Fay. As she sailed southward with her husband in the
pleasant autumn weather, her thoughts dwelt on the past
with irritation, on the future with hope, but on the
scenery scarcely at all. What with the boredom of
Alexandria, what with her fright at Cairo, what with
the native dress that fanaticism had compelled her to
wear ("a terrible fashion for one like me to whom fresh
air seems the greatest requisite for existence"), and
finally what with Suez, which she found "a miserable
place little better than the desert which it bounds", she
quitted Egypt without one tender word. Even her
Biblical reminiscences take an embittered turn. She
forgets how glad Jacob had been to come there and only

remembers how anxious Moses and Aaron had been to get away.

Content to have escaped, she turns her gaze within— not of course to her own interior (she is no morbid analyst) but to the interior of the boat, and surveys with merciless eyes her fellow-passengers. The letter that describes them exhibits her talent, her vitality, and her trust in Providence, and incidentally explains why she never became popular, and why "two parties", as she terms them, were at once formed on board, the one party consisting of her husband and herself, the other of everyone else. The feud, trivial at the time, was not to be without serious consequences. "You will now expect me, my dear friends," she begins, "to say something of those with whom we are cooped up, but my account will not be very satisfactory, though sufficiently interesting to us—to being there."

The grammar is hazy. But the style makes all clear.

The woman Mrs. Tulloch, of whom I entertained some suspicion from the first, is, now I am credibly informed, one of the very lowest creatures taken off the streets in London. She is so perfectly depraved in disposition that her supreme delight consists in making everybody about her miserable. It would be doing her too much honour to stain my paper with a detail of the various artifices she daily practises to that end. Her pretended husband, having been in India before and giving himself many airs, is looked upon as a person of mighty consequence whom no one chooses to offend. Therefore madam has full scope to exercise her mischievous talents, wherein he never controls her, not but that he perfectly understands to make himself feared. Coercive measures are sometimes resorted to. It is a common expression of the lady, "Lord bless you, if I did such or such a thing, Tulloch would make no more ado, but knock me down like an ox." I frequently amuse myself with examining their countenances, where ill-nature has fixed her empire so firmly that I scarcely believe either of them smiled except maliciously.

As for the captain, he is a mere Jack in office. Being unexpectedly raised to that post from second mate by the death of poor Captain Vanderfield and his chief officer on the fatal Desert, he has become from this circumstance so insolent and overbearing that everyone detests him. Instead of being ready to accommodate every person with the few necessaries left by the plundering Arabs, he constantly appropriates them to himself. "Where is the captain's silver spoon? God bless my soul, Sir, you have got my chair; must you be seated before the captain's glass?" and a great deal more of this same kind; but this may serve as a specimen. And although the wretch half starves us, he frequently makes comparisons between his table and that of an Indiaman which we dare not contradict while in his power.

Food is a solemn subject. Eliza was not a fastidious or an insular eater and she would gladly sample the dishes of foreign climes. But she did demand that those dishes should be plentiful, and that they should nourish her, and loud are her complaints when they do not, and vigorous the measures she takes.

During the first fortnight of our voyage my foolish complaisance stood in my way at table, but I soon learned our gentle maxim, catch as catch can. The longest arm fared best, and you cannot imagine what a good scrambler I have become. A dish once seized, it is my care to make use of my good fortune; and now provisions running very short, we are grown quite savages: two or three of us perhaps fighting for a bone, for there is no respect of persons. The wretch of a captain, wanting our passage money for nothing, refused to lay in a sufficient quantity of stock; and if we do not soon reach our port, what must be the consequence, Heaven knows.

Mr. Hare, Eliza's chief gentleman enemy, was not

dangerous at meals. It was rather the activity of his mind that threatened her. Whenever she writes of him, her pen is at its sharpest, it is indeed not so much a pen as a fang. It lacerates his social pretentiousness, his snobbery, the scorbutic blotches on his face, and his little white eyes. Poor young Mr. Taylor once showed him a handsome silver-hilted sword. He admired it, till he saw on the scabbard the damning inscription, "Royal Exchange." "Take your sword," said he; "it's surprising a man of your sense should commit an error; for fifty guineas I would not have a city name on any article of my dress." She comments: "Now would anyone suppose this fine gentleman's father was in trade and he himself brought up in that very city he affects to despise? Very true, nevertheless."

How, by the way, did she know that? Who told her? And, by the way, how did she know about Mrs. Tulloch? But one must not ask such dreadful questions. They shatter the foundations of faith.

And so his studied attention to me in the minutest article effectually shielded him from suspicion till his end was answered, of raising up a party against us, by the means of that vile woman, who was anxious to triumph over me, especially as I have been repeatedly compelled (for the honour of the sex) to censure her swearing and indecent behaviour. I have, therefore, little comfort to look forward to for the remainder of the voyage.

Then she reckons up her allies, or rather the neutrals. They are a feeble set.

It is only justice to name Mr. Taylor as an amiable though melancholy companion, and Mr. Manesty, an agreeable young man under twenty. Mr. Fuller is a middle-aged man.

He has, it seems, fallen into the hands of sharpers and been completely pillaged. He has the finest dark eyes I ever met with. Mr. Moreau, a musician, is very civil and attentive.

Small fry like these could be no help. They can scarcely have got enough to eat at dinner. Her truer supports lay within.

Having early discovered the confederacy, prudence determined us to go mildly on, seemingly blind to what it was beyond our power to remedy. Never intermeddling with their disputes, all endeavours to draw us into quarrels are vainly exerted. I despise them too much to be angry.

And the letter concludes with a moving picture of home life in the Red Sea:

After meals I generally retire to my cabin, where I find plenty of employment, having made up a dozen shirts for Mr. Fay out of some cloth I purchased to replace part of those stolen by the Arabs. Sometimes I read French or Italian and study Portuguese. I likewise prevailed on Mr. Fay to teach me shorthand, in consequence of the airs Mr. Hare gave himself because he was master of this art and had taught his sisters to correspond with him in it. The matter was very easily accomplished. In short, I have discovered abundant methods of making my time pass usefully and not disagreeably. How often, since in this situation, have I blessed God that He has been pleased to endow me with a mind capable of furnishing its own amusement, despite of all means used to discompose it.

Admirable too is the tone of the postscript:

I am in tolerable health and looking with a longing eye towards Bengal, from whence I trust my next will be dated. The climate seems likely to agree very well with me. I do not at all mind the heat, nor does it at all affect either my spirits or my appetite.—Your ever affectionate E.F.

She was to date her next not from Bengal but from

prison. Here, however, her Alexandrian audience must really have the decency to retire. Eliza in chains is too terrible a theme. Let it suffice to say that though in chains she remained Eliza, and that Mrs. Tulloch was enchained too; and let those who would know more procure "The Original Letters from India of Mrs. Eliza Fay", published by the Calcutta Historical Society. The book contains a portrait of our heroine, which quite fills the cup of joy. She stands before us in the Oriental robes she detested so much, but she has thrown back their superfluities and gazes at the world as though seeing through its little tricks. One trousered foot is advanced, one bangled arm is bent into an attitude of dignified defiance. Her expression, though triumphant, is alert. She is attended in the background by a maid-servant and a mosque.

COTTON FROM THE OUTSIDE

I

"Oh, Heaven help us! What is that dreadful noise? Run, run! Has somebody been killed?"

"Do not distress yourself, kind-hearted sir. It is only the merchants of Alexandria, buying cotton."

"But they are murdering one another surely."

"Not so. They merely gesticulate."

"Does any place exist whence one could view their gestures in safety?"

"There is such a place."

"I shall come to no bodily harm there?"

"None, none."

"Then conduct me, pray."

And mounting to an upper chamber we looked down into a stupendous Hall.

It is usual to compare such visions to Dante's Inferno, but this really did resemble it, because it was marked out into the concentric circles of which the Florentine speaks. Divided from each other by ornamental balustrades, they increased in torment as they decreased in size, so that the inmost ring was congested beyond redemption with perspiring souls. They shouted and waved and spat at each other across the central basin which was empty but for a permanent official who sat there, fixed in ice. Now and then he rang a little bell, and now and then another official, who dwelt upon a ladder far away, climbed and wrote upon a board with chalk. The merchants hit their heads and howled. A

terrible calm ensued. Something worse was coming.
While it gathered we spoke.

"Oh, name this place!"

"It is none other than the Bourse. Cotton is sold at
this end, Stocks and Shares at that."

And I perceived a duplicate fabric at the farther end
of the Hall, a subsidiary or rather a superseded Hell, for
its circles were deserted, it was lashed by no everlasting
wind, and such souls as loitered against its balustrades
seemed pensive in their mien. This was the Stock
Exchange—such a great name in England, but negligible
here where only cotton counts. Cotton shirts and cotton
wool and reels of cotton would not come to us if
merchants did not suffer in Alexandria. Nay, Alexandria
herself could not have re-arisen from the waves, there
would be no French gardens, no English church at
Bulkeley, possibly not even any drains . . .

Help! oh, help! help! Oh, horrible, too horrible! For
the storm had broken. With the scream of a devil in
pain a stout Greek fell sideways over the balustrade,
then righted himself, then fell again, and as he fell and
rose he chanted "Teekoty Peapot, Teekoty Peapot."
He was offering to sell cotton. Towards him, bull-
shouldered, moved a lout in a tarboosh. Everyone else
screamed too, using odd little rhythms to advertise
their individuality. Some shouted unnoticed, others
would evoke a kindred soul, and right across the central
pool business would be transacted. They seemed to
have evolved a new sense. They communicated by
means unknown to normal men. A wave of the note-
book, and the thing was done. And the imitation marble
pillars shook, and the ceiling that was painted to look

like sculpture trembled, and Time himself stood still in
the person of a sham-renaissance clock. And a British
officer who was watching the scene said—never mind
what he said.

Hence, hence!

II

My next vision is cloistral in comparison. Vision of a
quiet courtyard a mile away (Minet el Bassal), where
the cotton was sold on sample. Pieces of fluff sailed
through the sunlight and stuck to my clothes. Their
source was the backs of Arabs, who were running
noiselessly about, carrying packages, and as they passed
it seemed to be the proper thing to stretch out one's
hand and to pull out a tuft of cotton, to twiddle it, and
to set it sailing. I like to think that the merchant to
whom it next stuck bought it, but this is an unbridled
fancy. Let us keep to facts, such as to the small fountain
in the middle of the courtyard, which supported a few
aquatic plants, or to the genuine Oriental carpets which
were exposed for sale on the opposite wall. They lent
an air of culture, which was very pleasing. Yet, though
here there was no cause for fear, the place was even
more mysterious than the Bourse. What did it all mean?
To the outsider nothing seems more capricious than the
mechanism of business. It runs smoothly when he
expects it to creak, and creaks when he expects it to be
still. Considering how these same men could howl and
spit, one would have anticipated more animation over
the samples. Perhaps they sometimes showed it, but my
memory is of calm celibates in dust-coats who stood
idling in the sunshine before the doors of their cells,

sipping coffee and exchanging anecdotes of a somewhat mechanical impropriety. Very good the coffee was, too, and the very blue sky and the keen air and the bright dresses of some natives raised for a moment the illusion that this courtyard was actually the academic East, and that caravans of camels were waiting with their snowy bales outside. There were other courtyards with ramifications of passages and offices, where the same mixture of light business and light refreshments seemed in progress—architectural backwaters such as one used to come across in the Earl's Court Exhibition, where commerce and pleasure met in a slack communion. These I did not care for, but the main courtyard was really rather jolly, and that British officer (had he visited it) could certainly have left his comment (whatever it was) unspoken.

Hence!

III

In the final stage I was in the thick of it again, though in a very different sort of thickness. Cotton was everywhere. The flakes of Minet el Bassal had become a snowstorm, which hurtled through the air and lay upon the ground in drifts. The cotton was being pressed into bales, and perhaps being cleaned too—it is shocking not to be sure, but the row was tremendous. The noise was made no longer by merchants—who seldom so far remount the sources of their wealth—but by a certain amount of wooden machinery and by a great many Arabs. Some of them were fighting with masses of the stuff which was poured over them from an endless staircase. Just as they mastered it, more would arrive and completely bury them. They would shout with laughter and struggle, and then more cotton would come and more, quivering from the impetus of its transit, so that one could not tell which was vegetable, which man. They thrust it into a pit in the flooring, upon which other Arabs danced. This was the first stage in the pressing—exerted by the human foot with the assistance of song. The chant rose and fell. It was better than the chants of the Bourse, being generic not personal, and of immemorial age—older than Hell at all events. When the Arabs had trodden the cotton tight, up they jumped, and one of them struck the flooring with his hand. The bottom of the pit opened in response, a sack was drawn across by invisible agents, and the mass sank out of sight into a lower room, where the final pressure was exerted on it by machinery. We went down to see this and to hear the "cri du coton", which it gives when it can shrink no more. Metal binders were clamped round it and secured by hand, and then the completed bale— as hard as iron and containing two or three Arabs inside it for all I know—was tumbled away to the warehouse.

It is difficult to speak intelligently about or against machinery, and my comments made no great stir— *e.g.* "Why has it to be pressed?" and "Do the different people's cotton not get mixed?" and "What I like is, it is so primitive." To this last indeed it was somewhat severely replied that the process I had viewed was anything but primitive—nay, that it was the last word on cotton-pressing, or it would not have been adopted at Alexandria. This was conclusive, and one can only hope that it will be the last word for ever, and that for century after century brown legs and rhythmic songs will greet the advancing cataracts of snow. That peevish British officer would have forgotten his peevishness had he come here. He would have regretted his criticism of the Bourse. It was "A bomb in the middle of them is the only possible comment," and when he made it I realized that there was someone in the world even more outside cotton than I was myself.

THE DEN

At last I have been to a Den. The attempt was first made many years ago in Lahore City, where my guide was a young Missionary, who wasted all his time in liking people and making them like him. I have often wondered what he found to convert, and what his financial backers—old ladies in America and England—will have to say upon the results of his labours. He had lived in the Lahore bazaars as a poor man, and as he walked through their intricacies he explained how this became comprehensible, and that pardonable, and that inevitable, so soon as one drew close enough to it to understand. We did interesting things—went into a temple as big as a cupboard where we were allowed to hold the gods and ring the bells, visited a lawyer who was defending a client against the charge of selling a wife—and as the afternoon closed the Missionary said he supposed I should like to include a Den. He remarked that a great deal of rubbish was talked about opium, and he led me to a courtyard, round whose sides were some lean-to's of straw. "Oh! it isn't working," he said with disappointment. He peered about and pulled from a lean-to a solitary sinner. "Look at his eyes," he said. "I'm afraid that's all."

There my acquaintance with Vice stopped, until Egypt, the land of so much, promised new opportunities. It would not be opium here, but hashish, a more lurid drug. Concealed in walking-sticks, it gave delicious dreams. So I was glad of a chance of accompanying the

police of Alexandria upon a raid. Their moral tone was
superior to the Missionary's, but they had no better
luck. Advancing stealthily upon a fragile door they
burst it open and we rushed in. We were in a passage,
open to the stars. Right and left of it, and communicating
with one another, were sheds which the police explored
with their heavy shoulders and large feet. In one of them
they found a tired white horse. A corporal climbed into
the manger. "They often secrete bowls here," he said.
At the end of the passage we came upon human life. A
family was asleep by the light of a lamp—not sus-
piciously asleep, but reasonably disturbed by our
irruption. The civil father was ordered to arise and
carry the lamp about, and by its light we found a hollow
reed, at which the police sniffed heavily. Traces of
hashish adhered to it, they pronounced. That was all.
They were delighted with the find, for it confirmed their
official faith—that the city they controlled was almost
pure but not quite. Too much or too little would have
discredited them.

A few weeks later an Egyptian friend offered to take
me round the native quarters of the same town. We
did interesting things—saw a circumcision procession,
listened to an epic recitation—and as the evening closed
he asked me whether I should like to include a Den. He
thought he knew of one. Having laid his hand on his
forehead for a moment he led through intricate streets
to a door. We opened it silently and slipped in. There
was something familiar in the passage, and my forebodings were confirmed by the sight of a white horse. I
had left as an avenging angel, I was to return as a
devotee. I knew better than my friend that we should

find no hashish—not even the hollow reed, for it had been confiscated as an exhibit to the Police Station—but I said nothing, and in due time we disturbed the sleeping family. They were uncivil and refused to move their lamp. My friend was disappointed. For my own part I could hardly help being sorry for poor sin. In all the vast city was this her one retreat?

But outside he had an idea. He thought he knew of another Den, which was less exposed to the onslaughts of purity since it was owned by a British subject. We would go there. And we found the genuine article at last. It was up a flight of stairs, down which the odour (not a disagreeable one) floated. The proprietor—a one-eyed Maltese—battled with us at the top. He hadn't hashish, he cried, he didn't know what hashish was, he hardly knew what a room was or a house. But we got in and saw the company. There is really nothing to say when one comes to the point. They were just smoking. And at the present moment they don't even smoke, for my one and only Den has been suppressed by the police—just as his old ladies must by now have suppressed my Missionary at Lahore.

THE SOLITARY PLACE

DELICATE yet august, the country that stretches westward from the expiring waters of Lake Mariout is not easy to describe. Though it contains accredited Oriental ingredients, such as camels, a mirage, and Bedouins, and though it remounts to a high antiquity, yet I cannot imagine our powerful professional novelists getting to work at it, and extracting from its quiet recesses hot tales about mummies and sin. Its basis is a soft limestone, which rises on the seaward side into two well-defined and parallel ridges, and swells inland into gentle hills whose outlines and colouring often suggest a Scotch moor: the whole district has a marked tendency to go purple, especially in its hollows—into that sombre brownish purple that may be caused by moorland growths. Many of the bushes are like flowerless heather. In the lower ground barley is cultivated, and depends for its success upon an occasional violent thunderstorm which shall swill a sudden torrent off the hills. The ancients cultivated vines and olives here too, as the remains of their presses prove, and Cleopatra had a garden here, but from such luxuries the soil has desisted. It has beat a general retreat from civilization, and the spirit of the place, without being savage, is singularly austere. Its chief episode is the great temple of Abousir, which with its attendant beacon-tower stands so magnificently upon the coastal ridge. And inland lie the marble basilicas of St. Menas and his holy well. But these apart, there is nothing to catch the attention. The

tents of the Bedouins, so Mongolian in outline, seldom
cut the lines of the sky, but blend in colour with the
stone, against which they crouch. The quarries, vast
and romantic, lie hidden in the flanks of the limestone.
They do not play the part that a chalk-pit does in the
landscape of the Sussex downs. The place is not a
wilderness, it is a working concern. But it is essentially
solitary, and only once a year does it, for a brief space,
put its solitude away, and blossom.

There is nothing there of the ordered progress of the
English spring, with its slow extension from wood-
anemones through primroses into the buttercups of
June. The flowers come all of a rush. One week there is
nothing but spikes and buds, then the temperature rises
or the wind drops, and whole tracts turn lilac or scarlet.
They scarcely wait for their leaves, they are in such a
hurry, and many of them blossom like little footstools,
close to the ground. They do not keep their times. They
scarcely keep their places, and you may look in vain for
them this season where you found them last. There is
a certain tract of yellow marigolds that I suspect of
migration. One year it was in a quarry, the next by the
railway line, now it has flown a distance of five and a
half miles and unfolded its carpet on the slopes beneath
Abousir. All is confusion and hurry. The white tassels
of garlic that wave in the shadow of the temple may be
fallen to-morrow, the blue buds of the borage never have
time to unfold. The pageant passes like the waving of a
handkerchief, but in compensation without the lumber
that attends the passing of an English spring, no stalks
and reluctant exits of half-dead leaves. As it came, so it
goes. It has been more like a ray of coloured light play-

ing on the earth than the work of the earth herself, and
if one had not picked a few of the flowers and entombed
them in vases upon an Alexandrian mantelpiece, they
could seem afterwards like the growths of a dream.

It would require a botanist to do justice to these
flowers, but fortunately there is no occasion to do
justice to flowers. They are not Government officials.
Let their titles and duties remain for the most part
unknown. The most permanent of them are, oddly
enough, the asphodels, whose coarse stems and turbid
venous blossoms have disappointed many who dreamt
of the Elysian Fields. How came the Greeks to plant so
buxom a bulb in the solitary place they imagined
beyond the grave—that place which though full of
philosophers and charioteers remains for ever empty?
The asphodel is built to resist rough winds and to stand
on the slopes of an earthly hill. It is too heavy for the
hands of ghosts, too harsh for their feet, but perhaps ours
were not the asphodels the Greeks planted, and their
ghosts may have walked upon what we call Stars of
Bethlehem. The marigolds are solid too, but for the
most part the flora are very delicate, and their colours
aerial. There is a tiny vetch that hesitates between
terra-cotta and claret. There is a scented yellow flower
the size of flax which is only found in one part of the
district and which closes in the evening when the irises
unfold. Two of these irises are dwarf, and coloured
purple and deep blue; a third is larger and china blue.
There are tracts of night-scented stock. Down in the
quarries grows a rock plant with a dull red spire and a
fleshy leaf that almost adheres to the stone. As for the
shrubs, some have transparent joints that look filled

with wine; while from the woolly fibre of others jut
buttons like a blue scabious. Other blue plants wave
their heads in the barley. Mignonette, purple and
white anemones, scarlet and yellow ranunculus, scarlet
poppies, coltsfoot and dwarf orange marigolds, nettles
genuine and false, henbane, mallows, celandine, hen and
chickens, lords and ladies, convolvulus. English daisies I
do not remember. And many of these flowers are not
the varieties we know in England. The lords and ladies,
for instance, are smaller and thrust up their pale green
spoons in the open ground. While, to compensate, there
is a larger kind—an arum of great size with a coal-black
sheath and clapper—a positively Satanic plant, such as
Des Esseintes would have commanded for his con-
servatory. In this way, just here and there, the tropic
note is struck, and reminds us that these familiar and
semi-familiar flowers are after all growing in Africa,
and that those swelling hills stretch southwards towards
the heart of the dark continent.

But what impresses one most in the scene is the quiet
persistence of the earth. There is so little soil about and
she does so much with it. Year after year she has given
this extraordinary show to a few Bedouins, has covered
the Mareotic civilization with dust and raised flowers
from its shards. Will she do the same to our own tins
and barbed wire? Probably not, for man has now got so
far ahead of other forms of life that he will scarcely
permit the flowers to grow over his works again. His
old tins will be buried under new tins. This is the
triumph of civilization, I suppose, the final imprint of
the human upon this devoted planet, which should
exhibit in its apotheosis a solid crust of machinery and

graves. In cities one sees this development coming, but in solitary places, however austere, the primæval softness persists, the vegetation still flowers and seeds unchecked, and the air still blows untainted hot from the land or cold from the sea. I have tried to describe this Mariout country as it is at the beginning of March, when the earth makes her great effort. In a few days the wind may scratch and tear the blossoms, in a few weeks the sun will scorch the leaves. The spongeous red growth of the ice-plant endures longest and further empurples the hills. This too will dry up and the bones of the limestone reappear. Then all will be quiet till the first winter rain, when the camels will be driven out to surface-plough. A rectangle is outlined on the soil and scattered with seed barley. Then the camel will shuffle up and down dragging after him a wooden plough that looks like a half-open penknife, and the Bedouin, guiding it, will sing tunes to the camel that he can only sing to the camel, because in his mind the tune and the camel are the same thing.

BETWEEN THE SUN AND THE MOON

OF the three streets that dispute the honour of being Alexandria's premier thoroughfare the Rue Rosette undoubtedly bears the palm for gentility. The Bond Street (I refer to Rue Chérif Pacha) is too shoppy to be genteel, and the Boulevard de Ramleh competes from this particular aspect not at all. In its length, its cleanliness, and the refined monotony of its architecture, Rue Rosette outdoes either of its rivals. They are tainted with utility: people use them to get something or somewhere. But Rue Rosette is an end in itself. It starts in the middle of the town and no man can tell where it stops: a goal it may have, but not one discoverable by mortal leg. Its horizon, narrow but uninterrupted, ever unrolls into a ribbon of blue sky above the wayfarer's head, and the ribbon of white beneath his feet corresponds, and right and left of him are the houses that he thought he had passed a quarter of an hour before. Oh, it is so dull! Its dullness is really indescribable. What seem at first to be incidents—such as the trays of worthies who project from the clubs—prove at a second glance to be subdued to what they sit in. They are half asleep. For you cannot have gentility without paying for it.

The poor street does not want to be dull. It wants to be smart, and of a Parisian smartness. Eternally well-dressed people driving infinitely in either direction—that is its ideal. It is not mine, and we meet as seldom as possible in consequence. But friends of a higher social outlook tell me that, by a great effort, they can feel perfectly at home in the Rue Rosette—can transform the municipal buildings into Ministries, and the Consulates into Embassies, and arabias into broughams, can increase the polish on the gentlemen's boots and the frou-frou from the ladies' skirts, until the Rue Rosette becomes what it yearns to be—a masterpiece by Baron Haussmann, debouching in an Arc de Triomphe instead of a Police Station.

I have never been able to make that effort. When fancies do come here, they are of an older and friendlier civilization. I recall Achilles Tatius, a bishop of the post-classical period, who wrote a somewhat improper novel. He made his hero enter Alexandria by this very street one thousand years ago. It was not called the Rue Rosette then, but the Canopic Road, and it was not genteel or smart but presented throughout its length scenes of extraordinary splendour. Beginning at the Gate of the Sun (by the Public Gardens) it traversed the city uninterruptedly until it reached the waters of the Harbour (near Minet el Bassal), and here stood the Gate of the Moon, to close what the Sun had begun. The street was lined with marble colonnades from end to end, as was the Rue Nebi Daniel, and the point of their intersection (where one now stands in hopeless expectation of a tram) was one of the most glorious crossways of the ancient world. Clitophon (it was thus that the Bishop named his hero) paused there in his walk, and looked down the four vistas, over whose ranks rose temples and palaces and tombs, and he tells us that the crossways bore the name of Alexander, and that the Mausoleum close to them was Alexander's tomb. He does not tell us more, being in search of a female companion named Leucippe, whom he deems of more permanent interest, but there is no reason to doubt his statements, for Achilles Tatius himself lived here and dare not cause his characters to lie. The passage gleams like a jewel among the amorous rubbish that surrounds it. The vanished glory leaps up again, not in architectural detail but as a city of the soul. There (beneath the Mosque of Nebi Daniel) is the body of Alexander the Great. There he lies, lapped in gold and laid in a coffin of glass. When Clitophon made his visit he had already lain there for eight hundred years, and according to legend he lies there still, walled into a forgotten cellar. And of this glory all that tangibly remains is a road: the alignment of the Rue Rosette. Christian and Arab destroyed the rest, but they could not destroy the direction of a road. Towards the harbour they did divert it, certainly; the great thoroughfare contracts into the Rue Sidi Metwalli and becomes heaven knows what in the neighbourhood of the Rue des Sœurs. But in its eastern stretch it runs with its old decision, and the limestone and stucco still throw over it the shadows that marble once threw.

Of the two gates there survives not even a description. They may have been masterpieces of art, they may have been simple entrances, but they must certainly have included shrines to the god and goddess who respectively guarded them. No one took much notice of the shrines. Paganism, even in the days of Clitophon and Leucippe, was dead. It is dead, yet the twin luminaries still reign over the street and give it what it has of beauty. In the evening the western vista can blaze with orange and scarlet, and the eastern, having darkened, can shimmer with a mysterious radiance, out of which, incredibly large, rises the globe of the moon.

THE POETRY OF C. P. CAVAFY

MODERN Alexandria is scarcely a city of the soul.
Founded upon cotton with the concurrence of onions
and eggs, ill built, ill planned, ill drained—many hard
things can be said against it, and most are said by its
inhabitants. Yet to some of them, as they traverse the
streets, a delightful experience can occur. They hear
their own name proclaimed in firm yet meditative
accents—accents that seem not so much to expect an
answer as to pay homage to the fact of individuality.
They turn and see a Greek gentleman in a straw hat,
standing absolutely motionless at a slight angle to the
universe. His arms are extended, possibly. "Oh,
Cavafy . . . !" Yes, it is Mr. Cavafy, and he is going
either from his flat to the office, or from his office to the
flat. If the former, he vanishes when seen, with a slight
gesture of despair. If the latter, he may be prevailed
upon to begin a sentence—an immense complicated yet
shapely sentence, full of parentheses that never get
mixed and of reservations that really do reserve; a
sentence that moves with logic to its foreseen end, yet
to an end that is always more vivid and thrilling than
one foresaw. Sometimes the sentence is finished in the
street, sometimes the traffic murders it, sometimes it
lasts into the flat. It deals with the tricky behaviour of
the Emperor Alexius Comnenus in 1096, or with olives,
their possibilities and price, or with the fortunes of
friends, or George Eliot, or the dialects of the interior
of Asia Minor. It is delivered with equal ease in Greek,

English, or French. And despite its intellectual richness and human outlook, despite the matured charity of its judgments, one feels that it too stands at a slight angle to the universe: it is the sentence of a poet.

A Greek who wishes to compose poetry has a special problem; between his written and spoken language yawns a gulf. There is an artificial "literary" jargon beloved by schoolmasters and journalists, which has tried to revive the classical tradition, and which only succeeds in being dull. And there is the speech of the people, varying from place to place, and everywhere stuffed with non-Hellenic constructions and words. Can this speech be used for poetry and for cultivated prose? The younger generation believes that it can. A society (Nea Zoe) was started in Alexandria to encourage it, and shocks the stodgy not only by its writings but by its vocabulary—expressions are used that one might actually hear in a shop. Similar movements are born and die all over the Levant, from Smyrna and Cyprus to Jannina, all testifying to the zeal of a race who, alone among the peoples of the Eastern Mediterranean, appear to possess the literary sense and to desire that words should be alive. Cavafy is one of the heroes of this movement, though not one of its extremists. Eclectic by nature, he sees that a new theory might be as sterile as the old, and that the final test must be the incommunicable one of taste. His own poems are in Demotic, but in moderate Demotic.

They are all short poems, and unrhymed, so that there is some hope of conveying them in a verbal translation. They reveal a beautiful and curious world. It comes into being through the world of experience, but it is not experience, for the poet is even more incapable than most people of seeing straight:

Here let me stand. Let me too look at Nature a little,
the radiant blue of the morning sea,
the cloudless sky and the yellow beach;
all beautiful and flooded with light.
Here let me stand. And let me deceive myself into thinking
    that I saw them—
(I really did see them one moment, when first I came)
—that I am not seeing, even here, my fancies,
my memories, my visions of voluptuousness.

It is the world within. And since the poet cannot hope to escape from this world, he should at all costs arrange and rule it sensibly. "My mind to me a kingdom is," sang the Elizabethan, and so is Cavafy's; but his is a real, not a conventional, kingdom, in which there may be mutinies and war. In "The City" he sketches the tragedy of one who misgoverned, and who hopes to leave the chaos behind him and to "build another city, better than this." Useless!

The city shall ever follow you.
In these same streets you shall wander,
and in the same purlieux you shall roam,
and in the same house you shall grow grey. . . .
There is no ship to take you to other lands, there is no road.
You have so shattered your life here, in this small corner,
that in all the world you have ruined it.

And in "Ithaca" he sketches another and a nobler tragedy—that of a man who seeks loftily, and finds at the end that the goal has not been worth the effort. Such a man should not lament. He has not failed really.

Ithaca gave you your fair voyage.
Without her you would not have ventured on the way,
but she has no more to give you.

And if you find Ithaca a poor place, she has not mocked you.

You have become so wise, so full of experience,
that you should understand by now what these Ithacas
mean.

The above extracts illustrate one of Cavafy's moods—
intensely subjective; scenery, cities and legends all
re-emerge in terms of the mind. There is another mood
in which he stands apart from his subject-matter, and
with the detachment of an artist hammers it into shape.
The historian comes to the front now, and it is interesting to note how different is his history from an English-
man's. He even looks back upon a different Greece.
Athens and Sparta, so drubbed into us at school, are to
him two quarrelsome little slave states, ephemeral
beside the Hellenistic kingdoms that followed them,
just as these are ephemeral beside the secular empire
of Constantinople. He reacts against the tyranny of
Classicism—Pericles and Aspasia and Themistocles
and all those bores. Alexandria, his birthplace, came
into being just when Public School Greece decayed;
kings, emperors, patriarchs have trodden the ground
between his office and his flat; his literary ancestor—
if he has one—is Callimachus, and his poems bear
such titles as "The Displeasure of the Seleucid,"
"In the Month of Athyr," "Manuel Comnenus,"
and are prefaced by quotations from Philostratus or
Lucian.

Two of these poems shall be quoted in full, to illustrate

his method.* In the first he adopts the precise, almost mincing style of a chronicle to build up his effect. It is called "Alexandrian Kings" and deals with an episode of the reign of Cleopatra and Antony.

> An Alexandrian crowd collected
> to see the sons of Cleopatra,
> Cæsarion and his little brothers
> Alexander and Ptolemy, who for the first
> time were brought to the Gymnasium,
> there to be crowned as kings
> amidst a splendid display of troops.
>
> Alexander they named king
> of Armenia, of Media, and of the Parthians.
> Ptolemy they named king
> of Cilicia, of Syria, and Phœnicia.
> Cæsarion stood a little in front,
> clad in silk the colour of roses,
> with a bunch of hyacinths at his breast.
> His belt was a double line of sapphires and amethysts,
> his sandals were bound with white ribbons
> embroidered with rosy pearls.
> Him they acclaimed more than the small ones.
> Him they named "King of Kings!"
>
> The Alexandrians knew perfectly well
> that all this was words and empty pomp.
>
> But the day was warm and exquisite,
> the sky clear and blue,
> the Gymnasium of Alexandria a triumph of art,
> the courtiers' apparel magnificent,
> Cæsarion full of grace and beauty
> (son of Cleopatra, blood of the Lagidæ!),

* A third is on p. 55.

and the Alexandrians ran to see the show
and grew enthusiastic, and applauded
in Greek, in Egyptian, and some in Hebrew,
bewitched with the beautiful spectacle,
though they knew perfectly well how worthless,
what empty words, were these king-makings.

Such a poem has, even in a translation, a "distinguished"
air. It is the work of an artist who is not interested in
facile beauty. In the second example, though its subject-
matter is pathetic, Cavafy stands equally aloof. The
poem is broken into half-lines; he is spelling out an
epitaph on a young man who died in the month of
Athyr, the ancient Egyptian November, and he would
convey the obscurity, the poignancy, that sometimes
arise together out of the past, entwined into a single
ghost:

It is hard to read . . . on the ancient stone.
"Lord Jesus Christ" . . . I make out the word "Soul".
"In the month of Athyr . . . Lucius fell asleep."
His age is mentioned . . . "He lived years . . ."—
The letters KZ show . . . that he fell asleep young.
In the damaged part I see the words . . . "Him . . .
    Alexandrian".
Then come three lines . . . much mutilated.
But I can read a few words . . . perhaps "our tears" and
"sorrows".
And again: "Tears" . . . and: "for us his friends mourning".
I think Lucius . . . was much beloved.
In the month of Athyr . . . Lucius fell asleep . . .

Such a writer can never be popular. He flies both too
slowly and too high. Whether subjective or objective,
he is equally remote from the bustle of the moment, he
will never compose either a Royalist or a Venizelist

Hymn. He has the strength (and of course the limitations) of the recluse, who, though not afraid of the world, always stands at a slight angle to it, and, in conversation, he has sometimes devoted a sentence to this subject. Which is better—the world or seclusion? Cavafy, who has tried both, can't say. But so much is certain—either life entails courage, or it ceases to be life.

CONCLUSION

A SERIOUS history of Alexandria has yet to be written,
and perhaps the foregoing sketches may have indicated
how varied, how impressive, such a history might be.
After the fashion of a pageant it might marshal the
activities of two thousand two hundred and fifty years.
But unlike a pageant it would have to conclude dully.
Alas! The modern city calls for no enthusiastic comment.
Its material prosperity seems assured, but little progress
can be discerned elsewhere, while as for the past such
links as remain are being wantonly snapped: for
instance, the Municipality has altered the name of the
Rue Rosette to the meaningless Rue Fouad Premier,
and has destroyed a charming covered Bazaar near the
Rue de France, and out at Canopus the British Army
of Occupation has done its bit by breaking up the
Ptolemaic ruins to make roads. Everything passes, or
almost everything. Only the climate, only the north
wind and the sea remain as they were when Menelaus,
the first visitor, landed upon Ras el Tin, and exacted
from Proteus the promise of life everlasting. He was
to escape death, on his wife's account: he was not to
descend into the asphodel with the other shades whom
Hermes conducts, himself a shade. Immortal, yet some-
how or other unsatisfactory, Menelaus accordingly
leads the Alexandrian pageant with solid tread; cotton-
brokers conclude it; the intermediate space is thronged
with phantoms, noiseless, insubstantial, innumerable,
but not without interest for the historian.

E(DWARD) M(ORGAN) FORSTER, one of the foremost English writers, was born in 1879 of mixed English and Welsh ancestry. After attending Tonbridge School as a boy, he went on to King's College, Cambridge, with which his name was intimately connected in later years and of which he was for a time a Fellow. His writing is remarkable, among other qualities, for its convincing evocations not only of his native England but also of such scenes of his travels as Italy, India, and—as in the case of this book—Alexandria.

His books include the novels, *Where Angels Fear To Tread, A Room with A View, Howards End, The Longest Journey, Maurice,* and *A Passage to India; Marianne Thornton: A Domestic Biography; Abinger Harvest,* essays; and others.

E. M. Forster died in 1970.